THE

SCOT IN NEW FRANCE

AN ETHNOLOGICAL STUDY.

INAUGURAL ADDRESS,

LECTURE SEASON 1880-81.

READ BEFORE THE LITERARY AND HISTORICAL SOCIETY OF QUEBEC,

29th NOVEMBER, 1880.

BY

J. M. LeMOINE,

President, LITERARY AND HISTORICAL SOCIETY, Quebec;—*Délégué Régional de
l'Institution Ethnographique de Paris;—Membre Libre de la Sociéte
Américaine de France;*—Honorary Member of the HISTORICAL SOCIETY,
of St. John, N. B.;—Corresponding Member of the *Société Historique,* of Montreal;—of the *Institut Canadien,* of Ottawa;—
of the MASSACHUSETTS HISTORICAL SOCIETY;—of the NEW
ENGLAND *Historic-Genealogical Society,* Boston;—
of the STATE HISTORICAL SOCIETY, of Wisconsin, &c.

HERITAGE BOOKS
2024

HERITAGE BOOKS
AN IMPRINT OF HERITAGE BOOKS, INC.

Books, CDs, and more—Worldwide

For our listing of thousands of titles see our website
at
www.HeritageBooks.com

A Facsimile Reprint
Published 2024 by
HERITAGE BOOKS, INC.
Publishing Division
5810 Ruatan Street
Berwyn Heights, MD 20740

Originally published
Montreal:
Dawson Brothers, Publishers
1881

International Standard Book Number
Paperbound: 978-0-7884-3795-3

THE SCOT IN NEW FRANCE,

1535-1880.

Before opening as President the winter course of lec-
tures, I have a pleasant communication to make. Since
we last met, His Excellency, Lord Lorne, has honored
this Society, by becoming its Patron, during his term of
office.

LADIES AND GENTLEMEN,—In a paper headed " The
Component Parts of our Nationality," we strove some
time since to place on record the results of our
researches in Canadian History, and thus to dispel some
of the prejudices, entertained as to the origin of the first
settlers on Canadian soil. We felt a sincere pleasure in
laying before an enlightened public, the evidence which
reliable historians furnish, as to the birth and formation of
the nationality of the majority in the old Province of
Quebec, in order to demonstrate that the colonists sent out
by the French Monarchs and French Companies, unlike
those of St. Christophe and other French Islands, were
singularly free from blemish.

These ethnological studies, superficial as they may be,
we intend to prosecute, with respect to other factors in
our nationality : this evening we have selected a branch
of the subject, which though less familiar to us, is quite as
worthy of your attention ; the Scottish element in and
round Quebec.

A mark of distinction, as unexpected as it was unsoli-
cited recently bestowed on your humble servant, by the
Ethnographical Society of Paris,* renders still more ap-

---

* Mr. LeMoine, the bearer of a Diploma, as " Délégué Régional" for Quebec, of the *Institution Ethnographique de Paris*, wore for the first time, the *In-
signia* of this learned Society.

propriate he imagines, the selection of an Ethnographical subject, like the one which will engage our attention this evening ; without further preamble, we will venture to discuss this subject.

Under the title "Les Ecossais en France," &c., there appeared, some time since, a French work, in two robust quarto volumes—the result of twenty-five years of conscientious research by a French savant, Monsieur Francisque Michel. It purports to recapitulate, among other things, the career on French soil of Scotchmen, ever since the days of Wallace, ambassador to France, down to modern times. Monsieur Michel, of a certainty, has succeeded in investing with deep interest the enquiry he has originated.

With your permission, we will, to-night, attempt to investigate a cognate portion of his subject, from an ethnological point of view, using the light he has thrown on the aims and aspirations of Scotchmen in old France to follow the footsteps of their compatriots in New France— we mean, in the present Province of Quebec—heretofore, that of Lower Canada.

LADIES AND GENTLEMEN,—It shall be our aim to point out to you the traces left by Scotchmen, in Canadian history, in and round Quebec, from the dawn of Canadian history to modern times. In those sanguinary passages-at-arms, by land and by sea, which have made of our town and its environs classic ground, oft' shall we meet with the brawny descendant of Bruce and of Wallace, fearlessly brandishing dirk or claymore in the busiest part of the fray, his motto.

"Let us do or die."

Sandy, full fledged, is a many-sided individual. A man of war—we will also find him a successful tiller of the soil—leading in the mart of commerce—in the bank parlor—at the head of powerful trading ventures—in the wilds of Hudson's Bay—in the Editor's sanctum—in the groves of " Academe"—in the forum—in the Senate ; more than once " the observed of all observers"—at the top of the social ladder—his sovereign's trusted representative.

For all that, we dare not promise you, for the frugal, self-reliant Scot transplanted to the green banks of the St. Lawrence, such a seductive portraiture—such a glamour of romance—as surrounds the persevering and oft' adversity-taught soldier—successful diplomat—scholar—artist, &c., to whom Monsieur Michel introduces his readers on the vine-clad hills and sun-lit valleys of the Loire, the Garonne, and the Seine.

The arena of the Scot in Canada is more limited ; less attractive, the prizes rewarding success ; less far-resounding, the clarion of his fame on Canadian soil.

With every desire to enlarge our canvass to its utmost, we must be content to rest our enquiry, at the arrival on our shores of the first Europeans, in 1535,—that hardy band of explorers sent out by Francis I, and who claimed the soil by right of conquest, from the *véritables enfants du sol,*—the Hurons, Iroquois or Algonquins, of Stadaconé.

A crew of one hundred and ten, manned Jacques Cartier's three vessels : the *Grande Hermine,* the *Petite Hermine,* and the *Emerillon;* out of this number, history has preserved the names of eighty-one persons.*

Were Cartier's followers all French ? One can scarcely arrive at that conclusion, judging from the names and surnames of several. You cannot mistake where William of Guernesey "Guillaume de Guernese," hailed from. There is equally, an un-french sound about the name of Pierre Esmery dict Talbot. " Herué Henry," seems to us an easy transmutation of Henry Herué or Hervey. We once knew at Cap Rouge, near Quebec, a worthy Greenock

---

* The remainder having died, chiefly from scurvy, during the winter of 1535-6, on the banks of the River St. Charles. (See Appendix. Letter. A ,)

pilot whose name was Tom Everell; in the next genera-
tion a singular change took place in his patronymic; it
stood transformed thus : Everell Tom. Everell Tom, in
the course of time, became the respected sire of a numerous progeny of sons and daughters : Jean Baptiste Tom,
Norbert Tom, Henriette Tom, and a variety of other
Tom.

An ingenious Quebec Barrister, in a curious paper, read
at the annual Concert and Ball of the St. Patrick's Society
at Montreal, 15th January, 1872, has pointed out much
more startling transformations in some unmistakable Irish
names, to be met with in the Church Registers.

" Who could guess, asks John O'Farrell, that ' Tec Corneille
Aubry,' married at Quebec, on the 10th September, 1670, was an
Irishman ? Yet the Register leaves no room nor doubt upon the
subject; he was the son, says the Register, of " Connor O'Brennan," and of Honorah Janhour, of St. Patrick's (Diasonyoen),
Ireland, his real name being "Teague Cornelius O'Brennan."
In this connection, I may mention that, when I was pursuing my
studies in the College at Quebec, our Rector was the Rev. Dr.
Aubry, a worthy and pious Divine, and one of three brothers in
the Priesthood in Lower Canada, and the uncle of two other
young Canadian clergymen. Dr. Aubry, until quite recently,
lived in the firm belief that he was of purely French extraction;
in fact, if my memory serves me right, he used playfully, at
times, to pull my little ears for being, as he used playfully to
say, such a wicked little *Irlandais*. Now the researches of Father
Tanguay, in the musty old Church Registers of Lower Canada
have revealed the astounding fact that Dr. Aubry is, after all, a
countryman of our own, an *Irlandais*, a lineal descendant of that
Teague Cornelius O'Brennan; another of his descendants is
Parish Priest in the town of St. John's, near this city, Montreal.

Who, again, I ask, but one able to answer the sphinx, could
fancy that Jean Houssye *dit* Bellerose was an Irishman. He was
so nevertheless; was married here on the 11th October, 1671 ;
and as the Register attests, he was born in the Parish of St. Lawrence O'Toole, Dublin, and he was the son of Matthew Hussey
and of Elizabeth Hogan, his wife, both Dubliners and both under

the protection of that Irish saint, O'Toole. If I mistake not, Mr. Bellerose, the member for Laval, can trace back his pedigree to our friend Jack Hussey, from Dublin.

Thus also we find Jean Baptiste Reil, married at Isle du Pads, on the 21st January, 1704; he is surnamed "*Sansouci,*" which we may translate either "*careless*" or "De'il may care" as we please; this "Reil" is described in the Register as having been a native of St. Peter's Parish, in the City of Limerick, in Ireland; from the closeness of the dates, 1698 and 1704, from the singular nick-name (*sansouci*) he bore with his comrades, and from the consonance, "Riel" and Rielly, I should be inclined to think that our Isle du Pads friend was Jack Rielly, the de'il-may-care, all the way from Limerick, and that he must have taken and given some hard knocks under Sarsfield. This "Riel" or Rielly, as he should be called, is the direct ancestor of "Louis Riel" of Red River fame; and this fact may serve to account for the close friendship subsisting between Riel and O'Donohoe."—(*O'Farrell's Address*, 1872.)

It only remains to our antiquarian confrére to present Senator Bellerose and Louis Riel, with a shamrock on each St. Patrick's Day, so that they may not forget their newly fledged nationality.

Another of Cartier's companions rejoices in the name of "Michel Herué," this mightily sounds in our ears like Michael Harvey, one of the Murray Bay Harveys, of Major Nairn; amidst these now silent and shadowy discoverers of 1535, several names impress us as not being French. None remained in Canada, except those whom scurvy or accidental death struck down in their ice-bound quarters at Stadaconé,—opposite to where our city now stands.

Did any, and if so, how many hail from the Highlands or Lowlands of "auld Scotia"? Would you be surprised to find, in the days of Champlain, a full fledged Scot—an extensive landed proprietor—the father of a large family?

Who has not heard of the King's St. Lawerence pilot— Abraham Martin dit l'Ecossais? "Abraham Martin *alias* the Scot." Can there be any room for uncertainty about the nationaiity of this old salt*, styled in the Jesuits' *Journal,* "Maître Abraham," Master Abraham, and who has bequeathed his name to our world-renowned battle-field — the Plains of Abraham ? Mr. O'Farrell, how-ever, patriotically claims Martin as a fellow-country-man. When Admiral Kirke's squadron † in the name of Charles I took possession of Quebec on the 9th August 1629, Abraham Martin did not desert the land of his adoption, to return to France. He manfully stuck to the old rock. With his wife, Marie Langlois, his children and a few others—twenty-two all told, he seems to have cheerfully accepted the new *regime* which lasted three years.

Master Abraham, the Scot, for ought we know to the contrary, may have experienced but mild regret at seeing a new Governor of Scotch descent, Louis Kirke, the Cal-vinist, hoist his standard on the bastions of Fort St. Louis, evacuated by Governor de Champlain, who, on the 24th July, 1629, had sailed for England ; "more than one hun-dred of his French followers also sailed in a ship of 250 tons," provided by Capt. Louis Kirke, the new master of Quebec.

Whether he fraternised in any way with the new Gov-ernor or his protestant Chaplain, he fails to say: the "ancient Mariner" Abraham, a species of practical "Captain Cuttle," having like the rest of the French garrison, lived " on roots for months " previous to the capitulation, no doubt he took his fair share of the good things distributed —the food and raiment—liberally given out by Kirke, to that degree, adds Kirke's biographer, " that many of the

---

*Louis Kirke, was a brother to Sir David Kirke, William and Thomas Kirke. Louis a former wine Merchant at Bordeaux, was, by his father's side, of Scottish origin ; his mother was a native of Dieppe.

† The FIRST ENGLISH CONQUEST OF CANADA, by Henry Kirke, M. A., B. C. L. Oxon, London, 1871.

poor French and half castes, chose to stay under his command at Quebec, rather than undergo the horrors of an Atlantic passage," (*Page* 74). Scanty, however, are the annals of Kirke's administration, at Quebec, (1629-32).

His Reverence, the Chaplain, pays a visit to the Jesuits' residence, opposite Hare Point, on the St. Charles. They present him with paintings and books ; a mutiny breaks out ; the Chaplain was suspected of having a finger in it; Governor Kirke has him committed to prison.

In 1631, his services are sought to christen Monsieur Couillard's little daughter—the disciple of Luther performs the ceremony. Henry Kirke, the historian and descendant of Governor Louis Kirke, quotes from English State Papers, a curious inventory of the armament of the Fort (St-Louis) sworn to, on the 9th Nov., 1629, at London, by Samuel de Champlain, before the Right Worshipful Sir Henry Martin, Knight, Judge of the High Court of Admiralty (*Page* 75): there were, it seems, Martins in London as well as at Quebec in those days. We shall reserve this Inventory for another occasion.

The exhaustless research of our antiquarians has unearthed curious particulars about this Scotch sea-faring man—the number,* sex and age of his children his speculations in real estate†—his fishing ventures in the lower

---

* Anne, born in 1614.
  Marguerite, " 1621.
  Hélène, " 1627.
  Marie, " 1635.
  Adrien, " 1638.
  Magdeleine, " 1640.
  Barbara. " 1643.
  Charles Amador, " 1648, the first Canadian ordained as a Priest.

† A bequest in his favor of a lot of land at Quebec on the 15th August, 1646, by Adrien Duchesne, surgeon on board of M. de Repentigny's ship, which lot of land of twenty arpents, (afterwards named the Plains of Abraham,) had been conceded by the Company of New France to Adrien Duchesne, on the 5th April, 1639.

St. Lawrence ;* sometimes, we light on tid-bits of historical lore anent Master Abraham, not very creditable to his morality ; once, he gets " into chancery;"† as there is no account of his being brought to trial, let us hope the charge was unfounded ; a case of blackmail, originated by some "loose and disorderly" character of that period or by a spiteful policeman! On the 8th Sept., 1664, the King's Pilot closed his career, at the ripe age of 75.

Were Cartier's, were Champlain's Scots, the descendants of those adventurous sons of Caledonia, who, at an earlier date, had sought their fortunes in France, and had so materially helped to turn the scale of victory at the battle of Beauge, under Charles VII ? Who can ever tell ?

Those familiar with the history of the colony since its foundation, have doubtless noted the studied and uniform policy which once provided Quebec with French laws, French fashions, French officials, French soldiers and settlers, making it a species of close borough to other races, the natural result of the colonial policy of the period. They can scarcely expect to find many foreigners among its denizens under Champlain. Few indeed there were. Wolfe's conquering legions inaugurated an entirely new order of things. A Scotch face however might have been met with in our streets, before that era, and a pleasant one too. Five years previous to the battle of the Plains of Abraham, one comes across three genuine Scots, in the streets of Quebec—all however prisoners of war, taken in the border raids—as such under close surveillance. One,

---

* " Ce moys (juin 1648). Mre. Abraham, auec deux de ses gendres, s'en alla pour la 1ére fois a pesche des loups-marins ; il en prit la veille de la St Jean 42, a l'Isle Rouge, proche de Tadoussac, dont il fit 6 bariques d'huile."— (*Jesuits' Journal.* p, 111.)

† "Le 19 (janvier 1649) première exècution de la main du bourreau sur vne crèature de 15 ou 16 ans, laronesse. On accusait en même temps M. Abraham de l'auoir violée ; il en fut en prison, et son procès différé a l'arrivee des vaisseaux............."—(*Jesuits' Journal,* p. 120.)

a youthful and handsome officer of Virginia riflemen,
aged 27 years, a friend of Governor Dinwiddie, born in
Glasgow in 1727—had been allowed the range of the fortress, *on parole*. His good looks, his education, *smartness*
(we use the word advisedly) and misfortunes seem to have
created much sympathy for the captive, but canny Scot.
A warm welcome awaits him in many houses—the
French ladies even plead his cause ; *le beau capitaine* is
asked out; no entertainment at last is considered com-
plete, without Captain—later on Major Robert Stobo.
The other two are ; Lieutenant Stevenson, of Rogers'
Rangers another Virginia corps, and a Leith carpenter
of the name of Clarke. Stobo, after more attempts than
one, eluded the French sentries, and still more dangerous
foes to the peace of mind of a handsome bachelor—the
ladies of Quebec. He broke his *parole* and deserted. He
will re-appear on the scene, the advisor of General Wolfe,
as to the best landing place round Quebec :* doubtless,
you wish to hear more about the adventurous Scot.

A plan of escape between him, Stevenson and Clarke,
was carried out on 1st May, 1759. " Major Stobo met
the fugitives under a wind-mill, probably the old wind-
mill on the grounds of the General Hospital Convent.
Having stolen a birch canoe, the party paddled it all
night, and, after incredible fatigue and danger, they
passed Isle-aux-Coudres, Kamouraska, and landed below
this spot, shooting two Indians in self-defence, whom
Clarke buried after having scalped them, saying to the
Major ; " Good sir, by your permission, these same two
scalps, when I come to New York, will sell for twenty-
four good pounds ; with this I'll be right merry, and my
wife right beau." They then murdered the Indians'
faithful dog, because he howled, and buried him with his

---

* "He pointed out," say the Memoirs, "the place to land, where afterwards they did, and were successful."—(Page 70.)

masters. It was shortly after this that they met the laird of the Kamouraska Isles, le Chevalier de la Durantaye, who said that the best Canadian blood ran in his veins, and that he was of kin with the mighty Duc de Mirapoix. Had the mighty Duke, however at that moment, seen his Canadian Cousin steering the four-oared boat, loaded with wheat, he might have felt but a very qualified admiration for the majesty of his demeanor and his nautical *savoir faire*. Stobo took possession of the Chevalier's pinnace, and made the haughty laird, *nolens volens*, row him with the rest of the crew, telling him to row away, and that, had the *Great Louis* himself been in the boat at that moment, it would be his fate to row a British subject thus. "At these last mighty words," says the Memoirs, " a stern resolution sat upon his countenance, which the Canadian beheld and with reluctance temporized." After a series of adventures, and dangers of every kind, the fugitives succeeded in capturing a French boat. Next they surprised a French sloop, and, after a most hazardous voyage, they finally, in their prize, landed at Louisbourg, to the general amazement. Stobo missed the English fleet; but took passage two days after in a vessel leaving for Quebec, where he safely arrived to tender his services to the immortal Wolfe, who gladly availed himself of them. According to the Memoirs, Stobo used daily to set out to reconnoitre with Wolfe; in this patriotic duty, whilst standing with Wolfe on the deck of a frigate, opposite the Falls of Montmorency, some French shots were nigh carrying away his " decorated" and gartered legs, so comically alluded to in the Memoir.

We next find the Major, on the 21st July, 1759, piloting the expedition sent to Deschambault to seize, as prisoners, the Quebec ladies who had taken refuge there during the bombardment—" Mesdames Duchesnay and Decharnay, Mlle Couillard, the Joly, Malhiot and Magnan families." " Next day, in the afternoon, *les belles captives*, who had been treated with every species of respect were put on shore and released at Diamond Harbour. The English admiral, full of gallantry, ordered the bombardment of the city to be suspended, in order to afford the Quebec ladies time to seek places of safety."* The incident is referred to in a letter communicated to the Literary and Historical Society by Capt. Colin McKenzie. (1)

Stobo next points out the spot, at Sillery where Wolfe landed, and soon after was sent with despatches, *via* the St. Lawrence, to General Amherst; but, during the trip, the vessel was overhauled and taken by a French privateer, the despatches having been previously consigned to the deep. Stobo might have swung at the yard-arm in this new predicament, had his French valet divulged his identity with the spy of Fort du Quesne; but fortune again stepped in to preserve the adventurous Scot. There

---

* See *Journal du Siége de Québec*, 1759 ; J. G. Panet : p. 15.

(1) Extract from a Letter of a Volunteer in Wolfe's army, presented to the LITERARY AND HISTORICAL SOCIETY, by Captain Colin McKenzie, of H. M. 78th Ross-shire Buffs—Highlanders.

"On board of the STIRLING CASTLE, two miles below Quebec, 1759."

" The ravages of war are truly terrible, but may be rendered still more so, if cruelty grows wanton. Happily this is not the temper of Britons, whose natural humanity forbids their sporting with real distress. Some severity became necessary to curb the pride of an insulting enemy, and to convince them we were actually in earnest.

Hence proceeded those devastations already mentioned, which drew from the Governor of Quebec a sort of remonstrance, addressed to our commanding officer, with a menace to this effect. " That if the English did not desist from burning and destroying the country, he would give up all the English prisoners in his power to the mercy of the Indian savages." To this threat our spirited commander is said to have sent a reply to the following purport : " That his Excellency could not be unapprized of his having in his possession a considerable number of fair hostages ; that as to the prisoners he might do as he pleased; but, at the same time, he might be assured, that the very instant he attempted to carry his threats into execution, all the French ladies, without distinction, should be given up to the delicate embraces of the English tars.

N.B.—We have at least three, if not four transports, full freighted with French females ; some of them, women of the first rank in this country."

were already too many prisoners on board of the French privateer. A day's provision is allowed the English vessel, which soon landed Stobo at Halifax, from whence he joined General Amherst, "many a league across the country." He served under Amherst on his Lake Champlain expedition, and there he finished the campaign; which ended, he begs to go to Williamsburg, the then capital of Virginia."

It seems singular that no command of any importance appears to have been given to the brave Scot; but, possibly, the part played by the Major when under *parole* at Fort du Quesne, was weighed by the Imperial authorities. There certainly seems to be a dash of the Benedict Arnold in this transaction. However, Stobo was publicly thanked by a Committee of the Assembly of Virginia, and was allowed his arrears of pay for the time of his captivity. On the 30th April, 1756, he had also been presented by the Assembly of Virginia with £300, in consideration of his services to the country and his sufferings in his confinement as a hostage in Quebec. On the 19th November, 1759, he was presented with £1,000 as "a reward for his zeal to his country and the recompense for the great hardships he has suffered during his confinement in the enemy's country." On the 18th February, 1760, Major Stobo embarked from New York for England, on board the packet with Colonel West and several other gentlemen. One would imagine that he had exhausted the vicissitudes of fortune. But no. A French privateer boards them in the midst of the English channel. The Major again consigns to the deep his letters, all except one, which he forgot, in the pocket of his coat, under the arm pit. This escaped the general catastrophe, and will again restore him to notoriety, it is from General A. Monckton to Mr. Pitt. The passengers of the packet were assessed £2,500 to be allowed their liberty, and Stobo had to pay £125, towards the relief fund. The despatch forgotten in his coat, on delivery to the great Pitt, brought back a letter from Pitt to Amherst. With this testimonial, Stobo sailed for New York, 24th April, 1760, to rejoin the army engaged in the invasion of Canada; here end the Memoirs.

Though Stobo's conduct at fort du Quesne and at Quebec, can never be defended or palliated, all will agree that he exhibited, during his eventful career, most indomitable fortitude, a boundless ingenuity, and great devotion to his country—the whole crowned with final success.

" It has been suggested," say the Memoirs, "that Major Stobo was Smollett's original for Captain Lismahago, (the favored suitor of Miss Tabitha Bramble) in the adventures of Humphrey Clinker. It is known, by a letter from David Hume to Smollett, that Stobo was a friend of the latter author, and his remarkable adventures may have suggested that character. If so, the copy is a great exaggeration."

The Memoirs of Major Robert Stobo, printed at Pittsburg in 1854, were taken from the copy in the British Museum, chiefly through the instrumentality of Mr. James McHenry, an enterprising Liverpool merchant. Mr. James McHenry is a son of Dr. McHenry, the Novelist and Poet, formerly of Pittsburg."—(*Maple Leaves*, 1873.)

Monsieur Michel tells us that the Scots, in 1420, landed by thousands in France, to fight the English. In 1759, we shall also find some thousands in America, enlisted to fight the French. About that time great changes had taken place in Scotland. The disaster of Culloden, in 1745, had opened out new vistas. Fate had that year set irrevocably its seal on a brave people; the indifference of France had helped on the crisis. Scotchmen had had occasion to test the wise saying, " Put not your faith in Princes." The rugged land of the Gael had been left to itself to cope with the Sassenach. Old France was forgetful of her pledged friendship—of her treaty of 1420 ; what was worse—of more recent promises. This memory had rankled in the breast of the fierce " children of the mist," remarkable for their short tempers and long rapiers. Vain had been the appeal for assistance of the Scot, so liberal himself in the past of his blood on French battle-fields, to uphold the French banner ;—vain the cry for help uttered by the descendants of those faithful life-guards of Charles VII. Sandy has got the cold shoulder from his once cherished ally; his Highland blood is up ; revenge, he will have. Where is the time, when one of the royal line of Stewarts, John Stewart Earl of Buchan, at the head of 7,000 Scots and some French landed at incredible hazards at Rochelle, at the call of an ally, to meet the English at the battle of Beaugé, killing the English King's brother ? where, in the words of John's Mons-trelet, "the Duke of Clarence, the Earl of Kyme? the Lord Roos, Marshal of England, and in general the flower of the chivalry and esquiredom were left dead on the field,. with two or three thousand fighting men." France, in those days, knew how to prize the warlike Mountaineers. Buchan became a *Grand Connétable* of France—as high in fact as a Luxembourg or a Montmorency. In remote times, " next to the Royal family in France, were the houses of Hamilton and of Douglas, who almost rivalled them at home."—(Blackwood.) Scotch names abound on French soil, and Mr. Rattray notices some odd transformations.✱

✱" Of the Darnley Stewarts, there were Sir John, founder of the D'Aubignys, and Sir Alexander, who figures as " Vice-roy of Naples, Constable of Sicily and Jerusalem, Duke of Terra Nova," &c., also Matthew, Earl of Lennox, who sought the hand of Mary of Guise, widow of James V., and mother of Mary Stuart. His rival, oddly enough, was the father of that Bothwell " who settled all matters of small family differences, by blowing his son into the air." Of the nobility closely allied to royalty, there were the Earls of Dou- glas, Lords of Touraine, and the Dukes of Hamilton and Chatelherault. The Dukes of Richmond, Lennox and Gordon are, of course, entitled to the D'Aubigny dignity. Michel and the chroniclers give a host of Scottish names, most of them long since sunk in territorial titles, some of these may be noted as proof of the vast influence of the Scot upon the destinies of

A desire for revenge—such after the defeat of Culloden, was one of the motives stimulating the conduct of Highlanders with regard to France. Trusting to their swords and well-tempered dirks, they sought their fortunes on American soil, readily entering into the scheme to dislodge the French from Louisbourg and Quebec; in this deadly encounter, the ardent Scot shewed himself as true in his allegiance to Britain, as he had been to France when his faith was plighted and his arm raised, to smite the then traditional enemy of France—England. We are not how-

France. There are Guillaume Hay, Jacques Scrimgour, Helis de Guevremont (Kinrinmond) Andrien Stievart Guillebert, Sidrelant (Sutherland), Alexandre de Jervin (Girvin) Jehan de Miniez (Menzies), Nicholas Chambers, Sieur de Guerche, Coninglant (Cunningham), Jean de Hume, George de Ramesay, Gohory (Gowrie or Govrie) DeGlais (Douglas), D'Hendresson, Mauriçon, Dromont (Drummond), Crafort (Crawford), Leviston (Livingston) Bercy, Locart, Tournebulle, Moncrif, Devillencon or D'Aillençon (Williamson) Maxuel, Herrison (Henryson), Doddes, DeLisle (Leslie), DeLauzun (Lawson), D'Espence (Spence), Sinson (Simpson), &c., &c. The Blackwoods play a distinguished part, and there are also Thomas de Houston, seigueur and Robert Pittcloch, a Dundee man, and many others. These exiles from their native land, in fact regenerated France, at a time when the national pulse beat so feebly as to forbode dissolution, the hardy sons of the north impregnated the veins of France with their own vigorous Scotch blood. Like the Normans of England centuries before, the Scot colony " was received as a sort of aristocracy by race or caste ; and hence it became to be a common practice for those who were at a loss for a pedigree to find their way to some adventurous Scot, and stop there, just as, both in France and in England, it was sufficient to say that one's ancestors came in with the Normans."—(*The Scot Abroad*, Vol. 1, Page 93.)

" In all biographies of the great Colbert, he is said to be of Scottish descent. Moreri says that his ancestor's tomb is at Rheims ; Sully, whose family name was Bethune. Scottish enought of itself, though to trace relationship with the Beatons. Molière, to disguise the vulgarity of his pantronymic which was Poquelin, suggested noble descent from a Scot. Mr. Burton mentions that some Scots, who were petty landed proprietors in later times, found it to their advantage to use the prefix " de" before the name of their petty holding. John Law, of Lauriston, is a case in point, and the most ludicrous was an invented title palmed off upon Richelieu. Monteith's father was a fisherman upon the Forth, and when the Cardinal asked him to what branch of the Monteith's he belonged, the candidate for patronage boldly replied " Monteith de Salmonet."—(RATTRAY's *Scot in British North American, page* 213.)

ever here to sing the praises of the Scot, but merely to take· a glimpse of history.

Strange results flowed from the national disaster ; a few years subsequent to 1745, we find Scotchmen arrayed under different banners.   Whilst the Highlanders of the Master of Lovat took a pride and a pleasure in striking for King George II. in New France, their brethren-at-arms accepted commissions under the King of France, in Canada.. Thus Tryon—McEachren and the Chevalier Johnstone had sought safety in France against Tower Hill, and sailed (the latter as an Ensign) in 1748, from Rochefort,. with French troops destined for Cape Breton.   The Chevalier bears a name too well known in history for one to pass him over without a word of notice.   *Two Siege· Diaries and a Dialogue on the Campaign of 1759-60, in Canada, printed by this Society, are ascribed to Chevalier Jonstone ; his confidential appointment as Aide-de-camp· to General de Levis, at Beauport, during the summer of 1759, and the share he had in the engagement of the 13th· Sept. of that year, afforded him special facilities to see and describe the incidents of that memorable defeat.   The· previous career of the Scotch Jacobite had bëen exciting and full of adventure.   William Howitt furnishes the following pen-and-ink photo of the luckless Scot, who is,. as you are aware, the author of an interesting account of the disaster of Culloden.

" The Chevalier Johnstone's history is a romance of real life, to the full as interesting, and abounding with hair-- breadth escapes, as the tales of the author of Waverly ; and, indeed, frequently reminds you of his characters and incidents.   The chevalier was the only son of James.

---

1. * " The Campaign of Louisbourg, 1750-58—Quebec, 1867."

2. " A Dialogue in Hades, a parallel of military errors, of which the French and English armies were guilty, during the campaign of 1759, in Canada— Quebec, 1866 "

3. " The Campaign in 1760 in Canada—Quebec, 1866."

Johnstone, merchant in Edinburgh. His family, by descent and alliance, was connected with some of the first houses in Scotland. His sister Cecilia was married to a son of Lord Rollo, who succeeded to the title and estate in 1765. The chevalier moved in the best society of the Scottish capital, and was treated by the then celebrated Lady Jane Douglas with the tenderness of a parent. Educated in Episcopalian and Jacobite principles, on the first intelligence of the landing of Prince Charles Edward, he made his escape from Edinburgh to the seat of Lord Rollo, near Perth, where he waited the arrival of the Prince, and was one of the first low-country gentlemen that joined his standard. He acted as aid-de-camp to Lord George Murray, and also to the Prince ; and after the battle of Preston-Pans, he received a Captain's commission, and bore a part in all the movements of the rebel army till the defeat at Culloden. From Culloden, he escaped with the utmost peril to Killihuntly, where Mrs. Gordon, the lady of the house, offered to build him a hut in the mountains, and give him a few sheep to look after, so that he might pass for a shepherd ; but the uneasiness of his mind would not allow him to adopt such a life. He fled to Rothiemurchus, where the young laird advised him to surrender himself to the Government, as he had advised others, particularly Lord Balmerino ; advice which, had he adopted it, would have caused his destruction, as it did theirs. From house to house, and place to place, he escaped by the most wonderful chances and under all sorts of disguises. He passed continually amongst the English soldiers busy at the work of devastation, his blood boiling with fury at the sight, but instant death his fate if he gave one sign of his feelings. Seventeen days he remained in the house of a very poor peasant, named Samuel, in Glen-Prossen ; Samuel's daughter watching at the entrance of the glen. He was determined to reach Edinburgh if possible, and thence escape to England, and so to the Continent ; but the

chances were a hundred to one against him. Every part
of the country was overrun with soldiers, every outlet
was watched, and heavy penalties denounced on any
boatman who conveyed a rebel across the Tay and Forth.
He prevailed, however, with two young ladies to ferry
him over the Tay; but after a dreadful journey on foot
into Fifeshire, he found the utmost difficulty in getting
across the Forth to Edinburgh. The account of all his
negotiations and disappointments at Dubbiesides, where
no fishermen would carry him over; but where he did at
length get carried over by a young gentleman and a
drunken fisher, is very much in the Waverly manner.
After being concealed with an old nurse at Leith, and
partly with Lady Jane Douglas at Drumsheagh—he set
out for England as a Scotch pedlar, on a pony. On his
way he encountered a Dick Turpin sort of gentleman,
and again a mysterious personage, who entered the inn
where he was near Stamfold, seated himself at table
with him, and after playing away heartily at a piece of
cold veal, began to interrogate him about the rebels in
Scotland. Escaping from this fellow by the sacrifice
of some India handkerchiefs, he got to London, where he
lay concealed for a long time amongst his friends—fell into a very interesting love adventure—and saw many of
his comrades pass his window on their way to execution.
On one occasion he was invited by his landlord as a re-
laxation, to go and see two rebels executed on Tower Hill,
Lords Kilmarnock and Balmerino! He finally escaped to
Holland, in the train of his friend Lady Jane Douglas;
entered into the service of France, (in 1748) went to Louisbourg in America, and returned to France to poverty and
old age! Such is one recorded life of a Jacobite of the
expedition of forty-five." !

Chevalier Johnstone's Siege narratives also mention a
French post on the Sillery Heights (at Marchmont, Wolfe-
field or at Samos), commanded by an officer of the name

of Douglas—apparently a Scotchman. You will no doubt be surprised to hear of another Scotch name, within the precincts of the city before the capitulation, a high, very high, official—in fact, the French Commandant of Quebec, Chevalier de Ramezay.

Ladies and Gentlemen, there is no mistaking, the Scotch descent of the French commandant at Quebec, before the city capitulated. The *Lieutenant du Roy* was Major de Ramezay, one of four brothers serving the French King, three of whom had devotedly fallen in his service. Major de Ramezay, for his services had been decorated by Louis XV with the cross of St. Louis. His father, Claude de Ramezay, of the French Navy (*Capitaine d'une compagnie de troupes de la Marine*) had been two years Governor of Three Rivers and twenty years Governor of Montreal, under French rule: he died Governor of that city. More than three centuries back, the Scotch Ramsays had settled in France. The name of Ramsay is now well represented on our Judicial Bench. It will later on, again reappear among the Governors of Quebec. In 1820, the ancient Capital will welcome, to the *Château St. Louis*, George Ramsay, Earl of Dalhousie, a patron of education, a lover of history, and a friend to progress.

Nor was there any thing unsoldierlike in de Ramezay's surrender on the 18th Sept., 1759—It saved the despairing, devoted inhabitants from starvation, and the dismantled city from bombardment—from sack and pillage. The proceedings of the French Council of war, held before the capitulation and published under the auspices of this Society, has done the French Commandant effectual though tardy justice.*

---

* MÉMOIRE DU SIEUR DE RAMEZAY, *Commandant à Québec, au sujet de la reddition de cette ville, le 18 septembre 1759, d'après un manuscrit aux archives dela marine à Paris ; publié sous la direction de la Société Littéraire et Historique de Québec.* Québec—Des Presses de John Lovell, 1843.

The first British Governor of Quebec, a Scotchman, General James Murray, as it were, took loyally and bravely the keys of the city gates from the last French Commandant of the place, Major de Ramezay, of Scotch ancestry. There were more Scotch associated to the destinies of the old rock in those remote times than you are aware of.

Let us hurry on.

We feel as if we should never be forgiven were we to delay unfolding the warlike record of those terrible mountaineers of Fraser, at Quebec in 1759, so earnest in avenging on France's pet colony, France's indifference to the fate of their own country in its hour of trial.

> " Quebec and Cape Breton, the pride of old France,
>   In their troops fondly boasted till we did advance,
>   But when our claymores they saw us produce,
>   Their courage did fail, and they sued for a truce.
>   THE GARB OF OLD GAUL."

List of officers of Fraser's Highlanders, commissions dated, 5th January, 1757 :

Lieut.-Col. Commandant.—Honorable Simon Fraser, died Lieutenant-General in 1782.

Majors.—James Clephane; John Campbell, of Dunoon, afterwards Lieutenant-Colonel Commanding the Campbell Highlanders in Germany.

Captains.—John MacPherson, brother of Clunie.* John Campbell, of Ballimore; Simon Fraser, of Inverlochy, killed on the Heights of Abraham in 1795 ; Donald MacDonald, brother of Clanronald, killed at Sillery 1760 ; John MacDonnell, of Lochgarry, afterwards Lieutenant-Colonel of the 76th, or MacDonald's Regiment, died in 1789, Colonel; Alexander Cameron, of Dungallon ; Thomas Ross, of Culrossie, killed on the Heights of Abraham ; Alexander Fraser, of Culduthel ; Sir Henry Seton, of Abercorn, Baronet ; James Fraser, of Belladrum ; Simon Fraser, *Captain-Lieutenant*, died a Lieutenant-General in 1812.

Lieutenants.—Alexander MacLeod, Hugh Cameron, Ronald MacDonald, of Keppoch ; Charles MacDonnell, of Glengarry,

---

* See Appendix Letter B, Clunie MacPherson.

killed at St. John's; Roderick Macneill, of Bara, killed on the Heights of Abraham; William MacDonnell; Archibald Campbell, son of Glenlyon; John Fraser, of Balnain; Hector Mac-Donald, brother to Boisdale, killed in 1759; Allan Stewart, son of Innernaheill; John Fraser: Alexander Macdonell, son of Borrisdale, killed on the Heights of Abraham; Alexander Fraser, killed at Louisbourg; Alexander Campbell, of Aross; John Douglas; John Nairn; Arthur Rose, of the family of Kilravoch; Alexander Fraser; John Macdonell, of Leeks, died at Berwick, 1818; Cosmo Gordon, killed at Sillery in 1760; David Baillie, killed at Louisbourg; Charles Stewart, son of Colonel John Roy Stewart; Ewen Cameron, of the family of Glenevis; Allan Cameron; John Cuthbert, killed at Louisbourg; Simon Fraser, Archibald Macalister, of the family of Loup; James Murray, killed at Louisbourg; Donald Cameron, son of Fassafearn, died on half pay, 1817.

Ensigns.—John Chisholm; John Fraser, of Errogie; Simon Fraser; James Mackenzie; Malcolm Fraser, afterwards Captain 84th Regiment, or Royal Emigrants; Donald MacNeill, Henry Munro; Hugh Fraser, afterwards Captain 84th Regiment; Alexander Gregorson, Ardtornish; James Henderson; Robert Menzies; John Campbell.

Chaplain, Reverend Robert MacPherson; Adjutant, Hugh Fraser; Quarter-master, John Fraser; Surgeon, John McLean.

" Without estate, money, or influence, beyond the hereditary attachment of his clan, the Master of Lovat found himself in a few weeks at the head of eight hundred men, entirely recruited by himself. His kinsmen, officers of the regiment and the gentlemen of the country around, added seven hundred more. The battalion was thus formed of thirteen companies of one hundred and five men each, numbering in all one thousand four hundred and sixty men, including sixty-five sergeants, and thirty pipers and drummers—a splendid body of men, who afterwards carried the military reputation of the nation to the highest pitch. In all their movements they were attended by their chaplain, the Reverend Robert MacPherson who was called

by them *Caipal Mor*, from his large stature. They wore
the full Highland dress,† with musket and broadsword.
Many of the soldiers added, at their own expense, the dirk,
and the purse of Otter's skin. The bonnet was raised or
cocked on one side, with a slight bent inclining down to
the right ear, over which were suspended two or more
black feathers. Eagle's or Hawk's feathers were worn by
the officers. During six years in North America Fraser's

---

†William Skene, F.S.A. Scot, quotes *desly* (A.D. 1578) in speaking of
the Highlanders, ability to stand cold when clad in kilt and plaid—" *His
solis noctu involuti suaviter dormiebant. Reliqua vero vestimenta erant brevis
ex lana tunicella manicis inferius apertis, uti expeditius cum vellent jacula
torquerent, ac fœmoralia simplicima, pudori quam frigori aut pompœ aptioræ.*"
Wrapt up in these for their only covering, they would sleep comfortably.
The rest of their garments consisted of a short woollen jacket, with the
sleeves open below for the convenience of throwing their darts, and a covering for their thighs of the simplest kind, *more for decency than for show or a
defence against the cold.*"

In a lively newspaper discussion with the late Dr. W. J. Anderson, P. L. &
H. S., the question of the effects of climate on the kilted " Scots" in Canada in
1759 was discussed; we held forth as follows :

" Highland regiments as late as 1780, not only wore the kilt by choice but
exchanging it for any other dress, was in their eyes, positive degradation.
Regimental orders were found insufficient to do away with it. Nothing short
of an act of Parliament would effect it, and even that in some cases failed.
They appear to have held more staunchly to the kilt than to the Stuart
dynasty. An instance of this powerful national feeling of the Highlanders
occurred at Leith, about 1780. " Two strong detachments of recruits belonging to the 42nd and 71st Regiments, arrived at Leith from Sterling
Castle, for the purpose of embarking to join their respective regiments in
North America. Being told that they were to be turned over to the 80th
and 82nd,—the Edinburgh and Hamilton regiments who wore the Lowland
dress, they declared openly and firmly they had not been enlisted for such
regiments, and refused to join them. Troops were sent down, but the Highlanders flew to arms ; a desperate conflict ensued, in which Captain Mans-
field, of the South Fencible Regiment, and nine men were killed, and thirty-
one soldiers wounded. Being at last overpowered, the mutineers were carried
to the castle ; three of them were tried for mutiny. At their trial, they pleaded
first the difference of their language, the Gaelic, and also that they had been
accustomed to the Highland habit, so far as never to have worn breeches, a
thing so inconvenient and even so impossible for a native Highlander to do,
that when the Highland dress was prohibited even by act of Parliament,

Highlanders continued to wear the kilt both winter and summer. They, in fact, refused to wear any other, and these men were more healthy than other regiments which wore breeches and warm clothing."*

though the philibeg was one of the forbidden parts of the dress, yet it was necessary to connive at the use of it, provided only it was made of stuff of one color and not of tartan, as is well known to all acquainted with the Highlands, particularly with the more mountainous parts of the country."

The prisoners were sentenced to be shot, but the King subsequently granted them a .free pardon. It was stated in the work to which we refer that " *a great number of the detachments represented, without any disorder or mutinous behavior, that they were altogether unfit for service in any other corps than Highland ones, particularly that they were incapable of wearing breeches as part of their dress."

" Are we not, therefore, justified in replying to Lieut. Fraser, who, on the 20th December, 1759, appears to have been so concerned lest the stalwart mountaineers might catch cold, by reason of the wind's rude pranks with their kilts, in the words of one of the veterans. who had s een six North American winters, "Thanks to our gracious chief, (Col. Fraser,) we were allowed. to wear the garb of our fathers, and, in the course of six winters, showed the *doctors* that they did not understand our constitution ; for, in the coldest winters our men were more healthy than those regiments that wore breeches and warm clothing."

A Canadian peasant aptly remarked of the kilt that he considered it *"trop frais pour l'hiver, et dangereux l'été à cause des maringouins."*

J. M. L.

* THE KILT SUITABLE FOR WINTER.

(Quotations from the " Scottish Gael " by James Logan, Fellow of the Society of Antiquaries of Scotland.

" The hardihood of the Celtic race has been before noticed. Their dress inured them to the vissicitudes and severity of the climate. The lusty youth, says Marcellinus, had their limbs hardened with the frost and continued exercise."

" Pelloutier relates an ancedote, which shows how little this people regarded exposure to cold. One of their Kings, who was well clothed, one morning that the snow lay deep on the ground, perceiving a man laying down n aked, asked if he was not cold. 'Is your face cold ?' replied he—'No' said the King, 'Neither' returned the man, 'do I feel cold, for I am ALL FACE.' †

" The Highlanders, before the subversion of their primitive institutions, were indifferent to the severity of a winter night, resting content in the open air, amid rain or snow. With their simple breacan (plaid) they suffered 'the

*Browne's History of the Highland Clans, p. 183.
† Tome II, c. 7, from Ælian. Var. Hist. VII.

During the winter of 1759-60, a portion of Fraser's Highlandeɪ₀ were quartered in the Ursulines Convent. Whether the absence of breeches on the brawny mountaineers was in the eyes of the good ladies a breach of decorum, or whether christian charity impelled them to

---

most cruel tempest that could blow, in the field, in such sort that under a wreath of snow they slept sound.' The advantage of this vesture was almost incalculable. During rain it could be brought over the head and shoulders, and while other troops suffered from want of shelter, the Highlander carried in his mantle an ample quantity of warm covering. If three men slept together, they were enabled to spread three folds of warm clothing under, and six over them. The 42nd, 78th and 79th Highlanders who marched thro' Holland in 1794, when the cold was so severe as to freeze brandy in bottles, SUFFERED INCOMPARABLY LESS THAN OTHER CORPS WHO WORE PLENTY OF WARM APPAREL.

(*Extract from Morning Choronicle, Report of Lecture,* 1 *Dec.* 1880.)

" In order to fully illustrate the national dress and weapons, several members of the St. Andrew's Society having kindly offered the relics in their possession of yore the property of Fraser's Highlanders, in 1759, advantage was taken of their kindness Hon. D. A. Ross's dirk and skenedhu were conspicuous, among other antique curiosities. The sword produced by Mr. J. B. Dubeau, was of a slighter make than those of 1759—It dates back to 1776. Together with the sword of Brigadier General Richard Montgomery, Mr. James Thompson Harrower produced a Scotch blade—which had been the property of old James Thompson, his grandfather. It had on it seven heads of kings, wearing crowns. On the hilt of the dirk, was carved in the wood-work, the emblems of the Masonic craft. Mr. Thompson was very high in the craft. Among his papers there is one with an entry to the effect that a most cold-blooded murder was committed with this dirk, when his grandfather was at Rhode Island. It would appear that this Highlander had lent this dirk to an officer, who, happening to enter the guard room, was abused and violently assailed by one of his corps, a sergeant, who was intoxicated. The sergeant ended by seizing hold of his captain—throwing him on the ground, and before help came, despatching his superior officer with the officer's dirk, which he had plucked from its sheath."

Much discussion took place after the meeting, whether any of these swords were Andrea Ferraras—this style of sabre being common in 1759. After the lecture was over, some Highland "chiel" called on Mr. J. Doig, who had kindly consented to attend in full Highland costume, with the bagpipes. Mr. Doig played the " Reel of Tullochgorum " with great spirit, having next to him a gillie in full Highland costume, Mr. A. Watters' little son, Frank Stewart Watters. These little incidents heightened the interest in a subject effecting Scotch nationality discussed on the eve of St. Andrew's Day. The lecture room was crowded to that degree, that for many, there was but standing room."

clothe the naked—especially during the January frosts, is hard to determine at the present time ; certain it is, that the Nuns generously begged of Governor Murray, to be allowed to provide raiment for the barelegged sons of Caledonia.

Fraser's Highlanders distinguished themselves at the capture of Louisbourg, in 1758 ; at the battle of Montmorency, 31st July, 1759 ; and at that of St. Foy or Sillery, 28th April, 1760 ; a fitting tribute was rendered to their bravery on this occasion by the Hon. P. J. O. Chauveau, at the inauguration, in 1855, of the statue of Bellona, sent out by Prince Napoleon to crown the monument on the celebrated battle-field.

A singular incident marked the engagement at Carillon* on the 8th July, 1758, where a Scotch Regiment suffered fearfully.

"At the battle of the Plains, the loss of *Fraser's Highlanders* amounted to three officers, one sergeant, and fourteen rank and file, killed ; ten officers, seven sergeants,

---

* We read in Garneau, respecting the battle of Carillon, on the 8th July, 1758:

"It was the right of the trench works that was longest and most obstinately assailed ; in that quarter the combat was most sanguinary. The British Grenadiers and Highlanders there perservered in the attack for three hours, without flinching or breaking rank. The Highlanders above all, under Lord John Murray, covered themselves with glory. They formed the troops confronting the Canadians, their light and picturesque costume distinguishing them from all other soldiers amid the flames and smoke. The corps lost the half of its men, and twenty-five of its officers were killed or severely wounded." (*Garneau's History of Canada.*)

"Some Highlanders taken prisoners by the French and Canadians huddled together on the battle-field, and expecting to be cruelly treated, looked on in mournful silence. Presently a gigantic French officer walked up to them, and whilst exchanging in a severe tone some remarks in French with some of his men, suddenly addressed them in Gælic. Surprise in the Highlanders soon turned to positive horror. Firmly believing no Frenchman could ever speak Gælic, they concluded that his Satanic Majesty in person was before them—it was a jacobite serving in the French army." (*Maple leaves*, 1864, p. 102.)

(2) Manuscripts published under the auspices of the LITERARY AND HISTORICAL SOCIETY of Quebec, 1867-8.

and one hundred and thirty-one rank and and file wounded. The disproportion in the number of the killed to that of the wounded must be ascribed to the irregular and unsteady fire of the enemy, which was put a stop to on the charge of the British. Of the conduct of the Regiment on that eventful 13th September, an eye witness, Malcolm Fraser then a Lieutenant in this corps, has left an excellent narrative. From it we give the following extracts : After pursuing the French to the very gates of the town, our Regiment was ordered to form, fronting the town on the ground whereon the French formed first ; at this time, the rest of the army came up in good order. General Murray, having then put himself at the head of our Regiment, ordered them to fall to the left and march through the bush of wood towards the General Hospital, where they got a great gun or two to play upon us from the town, which, however, did no damage, but we had a few men killed and officers wounded by some skulking fellows, with small arms, from the bushes and behind the houses in the suburbs of St. Louis and St. John."

We shall interrupt this quotation of Lieutenant Fraser's journal, to insert some details, very recently furnished to us, by our respected townsman, John Fraser, Esq., better known as Long John Fraser ; * his memory is still green, despite the frost of many winters. " In my youth," says Mr. Fraser, "I boarded with a very aged militiaman, who had fought at the battle of the Plains ; his name was Joseph Trahan. In 1759, Trahan was aged eighteen years. Frequently has this old gossip talked to me about the incidents of the fight. I can well recollect, old Trahan used to say, how Montcalm looked before the engagement. He was riding a dark or black horse in front of our lines, bearing his sword high in the air, in the at-

---

* Our esteemed fellow townsman, now in years close on four score and ten, we regret to hear, lies on a bed of anguish at Charleston, S. C., with a fractured thigh.

titude of encouraging the men to do their duty. He wore a uniform with large sleeves, and the one covering the arm he held in the air, had fallen back, disclosing the white linen of his wristband. When he was wounded, a rumor spread that he was killed, a panic ensued, and the soldiers rushed promiscuously from the *Buttes à Nepveu* (near where the *Asyle Champêtre,*—now Mr. Dinning's house—stands), towards the *Coteau Sainte Genevieve* thence towards the St. Charles, over the meadow (on which St. Roch has since been built.) I can remember the Scotch Highlanders flying wildly after us, with streaming plaids, bonnets and large swords—like so many infuriated demons —over the brow of the hill. In their course, was a wood, in which we had some Indians and sharpshooters, who bowled over the *Sauvages d'Ecosse* in fine style. Their partly naked bodies fell on their face, and their kilts in disorder left exposed a portion of their thighs, at which our fugitives on passing by, would make lunges with their swords, cutting large slices out of the fleshiest portions of their persons. I was amongst the fugitives and received in the calf of the leg a spent bullet, which stretched me on the ground. I thought it was all over with me ; but presently, I rose up, and continued to run towards the General Hospital, in order to gain the Beauport camp over the bridge of boats. On my way, I came to a bake-house, in which the baker that day had baked an ovenful of bread. Some of the exhausted fugitives asked him for food, which he refused, when in a fit of rage at such heartlessness, one of them lopped off his head with his sword. The bloody head was then deposited on the top of the pile of bread. Hunger getting the better of me, I helped myself to a loaf all smeared with gore, and with my pocket-knife removing the crust, I greedily devoured the crumb. This was in the afternoon, and the sun was descending in the West."

The countless clan of the Frasers, in the length and

the breadth of our land, trace back to this grand old
corps, their kinsfolks across the sea and Simon Fraser's
companions-at-arms, the McDonalds—Campbells—McDon-
nells—McPhersons—Stewarts—Rosses—Murrays— Cam-
erons—Menzies—Nairns‖—Munros— McKenzies — Cuth-
berts, so deeply rooted in our soil. A descendant, the
Honorable John Fraser de Berry, of St. Mark, near
Montreal, in 1868, carried away by his gushing love of
country, set to work to reorganize the Clan, notwithstanding the inroads committed by time, intermarriages with
other races, loss of language, &c.‡ The scheme did not
succeed, and gave rise to many humorous comments.

‖ One of his descendants, the late seigneur of Murray Bay, John Nairn,
Esquire, married Miss Leslie, a daughter of the Hon. James Leslie, one of our
most respected public men. (See Appendix Letter C.)

‡ FRASER CLAN.

" THE "FRASERS" of the Province of Quebec, are respectfully requested to
meet at the office of Messrs. THOMAS FRASER & CO., at the Lower town,
Quebec, on SATURDAY, the twenty-fifth day of January, 1868, at TEN o'clock
A.M., to take into consideration the advisibility of organizing the " CLAN "
for the Dominion of Canada.

JOHN FRASER DE BERRY,	A. FRASER,
A. FRASER Senr.,	A. FRASER, JR.,
J. R. FRASER,	FRED. FRASER,
JOHN FRASER.	J. FRASER.

Jany. 21, 1868.   (*Quebec Morning Chornicle*, January 1868.")

THE CLAN OF THE FRASERS.

" At a meeting of the "Frasers" of the Province of Quebec, held at Mrs.
Brown's city hotel, Garden St., on the 8th February, 1868, Alexander Fraser,
Esq., notary, ex-Member for the county of Kamouraska, now resident in Que-
bec, in the chair ; Mr. Omer Fraser, of St. Croix, acting as Secretary.

1. It was unanimously resolved :
That it is desirable that the family of the "Frasers" do organize themselves
into a clan with a purely and benevolent, social object, and, with that view,
they do now proceed to such organization, by recommending the choice of
A Chief for the Dominion of Canada ;   A Chief for each Province ;
A Chief for each electoral division ;   A Chief for each County ;
A chief for each locality and township.

2. That the Chief of the Dominion of Canada be named "The Fraser," and
that he be chosen at the general meeting of the "Frasers" of all the provinces ;

The "Frasers" of 1759 and of 1775 readily courted danger or death in that great duel which was to graft progress and liberty on that loved emblem of Canada, the pride of its forests—the Maple Tree. If at times, one feels pained at the ferocity which marked the conflict and which won for Fraser's Highlanders at Quebec, the name of *Les Sauvages d'Ecosse*,† one feels relieved, seeing that the meeting was inevitable, that, the sturdy sons of Caledonia in Levis' heroic Grenadiers,* did find a foe worthy of their steel. Scotchmen, on the field of Ste. Foye, in deadly encounter

---

the said meeting to be held on the second Thursday in the month of May next, at ten o'clock in the forenoon, in such place in the City of Ottawa, as will then be designated.

To be the Chief of the Province of Quebec :

The Honorable John Fraser de Berry, Esquire, one of the members of the Legislative Council of the said Province, &c., being the fifty-eighth descendant of Jules de Berry, a rich and powerful lord (seigneur) who feasted sumptuously the Emperor Charlemagne, and his numerous suite, at his castle in Normandy, in the eighth century.

II. For the following electoral division :

Lauzon,—Thomas Fraser, Esquire, farmer, of Point Levis.

Kennebec,—Simon Fraser, Esquire, of St. Croix.

De la Durantaye,—Alexander Fraser, Esquire, farmer, of St Valier.

Les Laurentides,—William Fraser, Esquire, of Lake St. John, Chicoutimi.

Grandville,—Jean Etienne Fraser, Esquire, Notary.

Green Island, Stadacona,—Alexander Fraser, Esquire, Notary, St. Roch, Quebec.

The meeting having voted thanks to the president and secretary, then adjourned.　　　　　　　　　　　　　　　ALEX. FRASER.

Omer Fraser,　　　　　　　　　　　　　　　　　President.

　　　　Secretary.　　(*Quebec Morning Choronicle*, February 8, 1868.")

† The kilted Highlanders of 1759 were popularly known among the peasants as " *Les petites Jupes.*" Most exaggerated stories were circulated as to their ferocity. The following was one of the most accredited opinions :—"The Highlanders would neither give nor take quarter ; they were so nimble that no man could catch them, so nobody could escape them, no one had a chance against their broad swords. With the ferocity natural to savages they made no prisoners, and spared neither man, woman, nor child."

* A curious hand to hand fight between the Highlanders and French Grenadiers took place on the 28th April, 1760, at Dumont's Mill, on the site adjoining Mr. J. W. Dunscomb's house, on the St. Foye Road.

with France's impetuous warriors, doubtless acknowledged that the latter were not unworthy descendants of
those whom they had helped to rout England's soldiery
at the fields of Beaugé, Crevant and Verneuil.

Scurvy and salt provisions had decimated the ranks of
Fraser's men, during that same winter of 1759-60. The
regiment went into action on 28th April, 1760, under very
depressing circumstances; still the martial ardour of other
days burned fiercely in their breasts.

As previously stated, Fraser's 78th Highlanders after the
war was over, were disbanded, in 1764 : the Volunteers
had settled here in 1762, and, later, in the Maritime provinces.

You think, perhaps, you have seen the last of the
Sauvages d'Ecosse. Far from it; a new opportunity for
the display of their martial qualities is close at hand.
Barely sixteen years will suffice to bring it round.

Across our borders a great agitation reigned in 1775.
An unwise, nay, an unjust policy; taxation without
representation—has roused all New England; the wave
of invasion threatens Canadian homes. King George calls
to arms all his Canadian lieges, the *old* as well as the *new*
subjects, whose allegiance barely counts sixteen summers.
One and all respond, despite threats or seductive promises;—none more so, than the gallant Fraser's Highlanders, settled in Canada.

In an incrediable short delay, as if by magic, a Regiment,

" With this old windmill is associated one of the most thrilling episodes of
the conflict. Some of the French Grenadiers and some of Fraser's Highlanders took, lost and re-took the Mill three times, their respective officers looking on in mute astonishment and admiration ; *whilst a Scotch piper, who had been
under arrest for bad conduct, ever since the* 13th *Sept.,* 1759, *was piping away within
hearing :*—so says an old Chronicle—*Maple Leaves,* 1873, p. 182.

See Appendix Letter D.

the 84th* or *Royal Emigrants*, with recruits from Prince Edward Island, Newfoundland, &c., sprung up, under Lt.-Colonel Allan McLean, of the late 104th Highland Regiment, Captains Malcolm and Hugh Fraser, late of the 78th. This corps was installed in our "grim and stern keep, which watches over the city." Such is the confidence placed in the skill and bravery of Colonel McLean that the staunch little garrison, 1,800 strong, is placed under his orders by Sir Guy Carleton. During the agony of that dreadful winter of siege, famine, small pox, with traitors in and out of the city; with Crown Point, Fort St. John, Chambly, Montreal, Sorel, Three Rivers, in fact every foot of ground round Quebec (except that enclosed by the walls) in the possession of the New England and New York soldiery, the Scotch commander was found to be "the right man in the right place." Aided by the Regulars—by the Canadian Militia, under brave Colonels Dupré and La Maitre,—by the English Militia under Col. Henry Caldwell,—by British seamen, Masters and Mates, led by Capt. McKenzie and Capt. Hamilton, Col. McLean, under the eye of Guy Carleton, proudly upheld the banner of Merry England on the bastions of Quebec, but there only in all New France. Once the flag of Britain was firmly implanted in Canada, the Scot turned his mind to new fields of enterprise—to commerce and the tilling of the soil.

'Tis a pleasing spectacle to witness, later on, the substantial acknowledgment of services rendered, made by

---

* Two Battalions—Embodied in 1775—Regimented in 1778.

"1st battalion was to be raised from the Highland Emigrants in Canada, and the discharged men of the 42nd, of Fraser's and Montgomery's Highlanders who had settled in North America after the peace of 1763. Lieut-Colonel Allan McLean (son of Forlish) of the late 104th Highland Regiment was appointed Lieut-Colonel Commandant of the 1st battalion. The men of the 1st battalion settled in Canada; those of the 2nd in Nova Scotia, forming a settlement which they named Douglas. Many of the officers, however, returned home."—(Brown's History of the Highlands, vol. IV., p. 309.

the British Government, in grants of land to Scotch soldiers. Valuable seigniories are conceded to their officers; thus, Major Nairn, of the *Royal Emigrants*, received a patent for the *Fief* of Murray Bay, on the Lower St. Lawrence, while his companion-at-arms, Lieutenant Malcolm Fraser, had, on 27th April, 1762, obtained the adjoining seigniory, Mount Murray, bounded to the west by the river Murray or Mal Baie, to the east by the Rivière Noire—running three leagues into the interior.

Their followers and retainers crowded around them; soon a whole Scotch colony flourished round the bay or on the highlands of this picturesque spot, which in many particulars reminds one of the glens and gorges of Scotland : to this day many hamlets resound with the names of McLean, McNichol, Blackburn, Warren, Harvey, McNiell, old 78th men, albeit the name only now survives. Alliances with the French Canadian peasantry, have obliterated all trace of a Celtic nationality, though the descendants of the famous Lairds of 1762, Major Nairn and Lieut. Fraser still hold their own in their snug and solid old Manors. Fraser's Highlanders settled all over Lower Canada ; their descendants now number (it is said) more than 3,000. Scarcely a parish in the Lower St. Lawrence without some off-shoot from the parent tree : at Levis, Beaumont, St. Michel, St. Vallier, St. François, St. Thomas, St. André, Rivière-du-Loup, Restigouche, Matapedia, &c.

There are, however, populous settlements of Scotch— such as that of Metis—which do not hail from the Fraser Highlanders. This colony was formed in 1823, by the late J. McNider of Quebec. There are wealthy Scots in the Baie des Chaleurs, who do not trace either to Fraser's Highlanders or to the U. E. Loyalists of 1783—such as the Laird of Cluny Cottage, Wm. McPherson, Esq., for thirty-four years Mayor of Port Daniel, and who had settled there in 1838. ✱

Several Scotch United Empire Loyalists, in 1783, coming from the adjacent United States Provinces, settled at the Baie des Chaleurs, as well as at New Carlisle, under the predecessors of Lieut.-Governor Major Nicholas Cox ; at Sorel—on the Bay of Quinté,—at Douglastown on Gaspé Bay ; at the latter place, the seignior of Crane Island, in 1803, Daniel McPherson, Esq., † had settled about 1790 with the Annetts, Coffins, Murisons, Kennedys, and other U. E. Loyalists.

Many are the ethnological changes, in Lower Canada, ushered in by British rule : and with the experience of the past, varied indeed will be in a hundred years hence the rich concrete, composing our nationality, if the blind God of love should continue to shoot his darts in defiance of race, language or creed.

If Sandy shewed a *penchant* for the bright eyed Josettes of New France, French families even those with the bluest blood, were not averse to Scotch or English alliances ; in proof whereof, you will find at the end of this paper a list of military marriages and some ethnological notes which may startle you.

---

* Born on the 14th October, 1808, in Invernesshire, Scotland, not far from the field of Culloden, and emigrated with his family to the *Baie des Chaleurs* in 1819. Was elected mayor of Port Daniel in 1843 and continued mayor until 1877.—34 years.

† Daniel McPherson, a noted U. E. Loyalist, born at Inverness, Scotland in 1752, resided at Sorel first, where he married a Miss Kelly : he left Sorel some time about 1790 for Douglastown, Gaspé ; engaged in the fisheries and in agricultural pursuits with success, opened subsequently a large fishery stand at Point St. Peter, Gaspé ; he died at St. Thomas, Montmagny, in June, 1840, aged 88 years. The lecturer, whose youth was spent under his grandfather's hospitable roof from 1828 to 1838, by his mother Miss M. McPherson, is the grand-son of this respected old U. E. Loyalist, after whom he was named James (McPherson) LeMoine : his French ancestors hailed from Pistre, near Rouen, in Normandy, and were closely connected with the other celebrated Norman family, LeMoine de Longueuil.

The widow of the third Baron de Longueil Charles Jacques LaMoine gave her hand in marriage at Montreal, on the 11th September, 1770, to the Hon. William Grant, Receiver General of the Province, while on the 7th May, 1781, Capt. David Alexander Grant, a nephew of the Hon. W. Grant, led to the altar her daughter, who subsequently assumed the title of Baroness de Longueuil; Charles Colmore Grant, a lineal descendant, now inherits the Baronial title in Canada by warrant of H. M. Queen Victoria, published in the *London Gazette*, * of 7th Dec. 1880.

Later on, we find the haughty Scotch family of Lennox† connected by marriage with the proud and warlike family of LaCorne de St. Luc.

It furnishes quite a curious study to follow the chain of events, and to see how antipathies of race fade away before the harmonizing influence of Hymen. Scotch as well as English officers, of Montreal and Quebec, are united to the best French blood in the colony : thus we have such noted names as DeGaspé, Duchesnay, de St. Ours, DeSalaberry, Panet, LeMoine, de Longueuil, de Montenach, Coursol, Sicotte, Duval, Chauveau, changing to Stuart, Fraser, Campbell, Hatt, Herbert, McPherson,

---

* This graceful recognition of the most distinguished French house in Canada is republished under authority of the Dominion Government in the *Canada Gazette*, of 22nd January 1881, as follows :

Extract from the London Gazette of the 7th day of December, 1880.

DOWNING STREET, December 4, 1880.

"The Queen has been graciously pleased to recognize the claim of Charles Colmore Grant, Esq., to the title of Baron de Longueuil, in the Province of Quebec, Canada.

This title was conferred upon his ancestor, Charles le Moine : by Letters Patent of Nobility, signed by King Louis XIV, in the year 1700."

† Miss M. Lennox was a daughter of Major the Earl of Lennox, son of the Duke of Richmond and Aubigny, and of Mademoiselle Marguerite Lacorne de Chapt de St. Luc—a family equally distinguished on Canadian battle fields and among the French noblemen. After the death of Earl Lennox his widow married Le Commandant Jacques Viger, the Montreal antiquarian. A detailed obituary notice of Madame Viger appeared in the Montreal "Minerve."

Shakespeare, Smythe, White, Kane, Worseley, Serocold, Glendonwyn.

So far, it has been our task to sketch the career of Scotchmen in Canada, placed in subordinate positions; we will now, with your leave, view them in those exalted offices to which their sovereign may call them. We shall therefore point out a few only of our rulers of Scotch nationality ; the first was General James Murray, fourth son of Lord Elibank, and first British Governor of Quebec by the departure of the Marquis of Townshend.

General Murray, by his cool bravery, had won the respect of all parties. If the check his impetuous valor at the battle of Ste. Foye, subjected him to, for a time earned for him the epithet of "rash,"*it never cast a slur, either on his courage in action, or his wisdom as an able and humane administrator. Murray seems to have made the same mistake as Montcalm had done ; rushing out with inferior forces to meet the enemy, not trusting to the fortifications of Quebec. Though he was much outnumbered on the 28th April, 1760, it must not be forgotten that he occupied a good position on the Ste. Foye and St. Louis heights, with an excellent park of artillery, in all twenty-two guns, while the French had but two. Here again, Fraser's Highlanders previously decimated by famine and scurvy, but unsubdued, shed liberally their life-blood. For the French it was a brilliant, but bootless victory, and one which merely allowed them, on leaving the country, to shake hands as equals with their brave opponents.

Murray held his own in the city, despite the pursuit of a valiant foe flushed with victory. Relief came early in May following ; and with Lord Amherst, on the 8th September 1760, he completed the subjugation of Canada by the capitulation of Montreal.

* See Appendix Letter E.

On his return to England, he was rewarded by a higher command. "General Murray, says his biographer, was subsequently distinguished for his gallant, though unsuccessful defence of Minorca, in 1781, against the Duc de Crillon, at the head of a large Spanish and French force. De Crillon, despairing of success, endeavored to corrupt the trusty and gallant Scot, offering him the sum of one million sterling for the surrender of the fortress. Indignant at this attempt, General Murray immediately addressed the following letter to the Duke:

"Fort St. Phillip, 16th October, 1781.

When your brave ancestor was desired by his sovereign to assassinate the Duke de Guise, he returned the answer which you should have thought of, when you attempted to assassinate the character of a man whose birth is as illustrious as your own, or that of the Duke de Guise. I can have no further communication with you but in arms. If you have any humanity, pray send clothing for your unfortunate prisoners in my possession; leave it at a distance to be taken up for them, because I will admit of no contact for the future, but such as is hostile in the most inveterate degree."

There is a true ring here! One feels better after reading such sentiments. You cannot mistake that proud sense of duty, which had actuated the Scot on French soil, three centuries previous,—death preferable to dishonor—a sentiment which had won for him the well known epithet, "Fier comme un Ecossais."

The Duke de Crillon's reply was characteristic:

"Your letter, said he, restores each of us to our places; it confirms me in the high opinion I have always had of you. I accept your last proposal with pleasure."

General James Murray, closed his career in 1791 and was buried in Westminster Abbey. Haydn adds that after his death, on his corpse being opened for the purpose of being embalmed, many bullets by which he had been wounded last in Germany and Canada, were extracted.

"Of the Scots connected with Canada during the period from the conquest to the war of 1812, there are some who seem to require special notice. One of these was Sir William Grant, the third Attorney General of Quebec, born in 1754, at Elchies on the Spray, in the North of Scotland. His distinguished judical career has no connection with Canada, and he was only temporarily a resident in this country, during a brief period from 1776. When he returned home, Lord Thurlow said of him : " Be not surprised if.that young man should one day occupy this seat,"—and it is stated that he might have occupied the wool-sack but refused it. He filled high judical offices in England, being successively Lord Chief Justice of the Common Pleas and Master of the Rolls." RATTRAY'S *Scot in British North America, P.* 313.)

Later on, two eminent Scotchmen found a resting place in the vaults of the English Cathedral at Quebec. Lieut. Governor Peter Hunter, in 1805, the brother of two celebrated physicians, John and William Hunter ; and our then Governor-in-Chief, the Duke of Richmond, on 4th September 1819.

In that long list of Viceroys charged with the administration of Canada from our first Scotch Governor Murray, to our present, the Marquis of Lorne, more than one exhibited the distinctive, the most commendable traits of the Scotch character. In the critical times of the first Empire, in 1807, when England, in addition to her gigantic struggle with Napoleon I, expected (and was not disappointed) a war with the United States, the reins of office, in Canada were confided to a Scotchman, General Sir James Craig ; and if there were faults in the tried old soldier, 'twas not want of nerve, want of back-bone, in the hour of danger. †

† See Appendix Letter F.

Later on, when the ashes of insurrection were still hot, and the commonwealth required a firm but humane hand to allay civic strife, another Scot—a descendant of the Bruce—James, Earl of Elgin, was sent out. This* brilliant orator and successful statesman lived to see his arduous mission on Canadian soil rewarded by his Sovereign; high diplomatic functions were entrusted to him in China and Japan ; his courage and foresight, on the breaking out of the Indian mutiny in 1857, by daring in the nick of time, to divert from China the British expeditionary forces sent out and ordering them to Calcutta, 'twas thought, saved India to England.

---

* In September, 1851, in company with a much respected friend, F. X. Garneau, the Canadian historian, and a crowd of guests invited to the Boston Jubilee, it was our good fortune to attend the great civic entertainment tendered in the Boston Common, by the hospitable city Government of Boston to Lord Elgin his Cabinet and twenty thousand guests. Though several of the master minds of the Great Republic, Hon. Daniel Webster, Hon. Mr. Everett, Mr. Putnam and others, entranced their many hearers by their powerful or graceful oratory, we can yet recall the sentiments of pleasure with which the audience, and of pride, with which ourselves in particular, listened to the flowing periods of our Vice-Roy. It was not the first, it was not the last triumph his eloquence achieved on United States Territory.

His able biographer furnishes the following anecdote : " Some years afterwards, says Walrond, when speaking of these festivities, the Mayor of Buffalo said : " Never shall I forget the admiration elicited by Lord Elgin's beautiful speech on that occasion. Upon the American visitors (who it must be confessed, do not look for the highest order of intellect in the appointees of the Crown) the effect was amusing. A sterling Yankee friend, while the Governor was speaking, sat by my side, and occasionally gave vent to his feelings as the speech progressed, each sentence increasing in beauty and eloquence, by such approving exclamations as " He's a glorious fellow ! He ought to be on our side of the line ! We would make him mayor of our city ! " As some new burst of eloquence breaks from the speaker's lips, my worthy friend exclaims " How magnificently he talks ! Yes, by George ! we'd make him governor, governor of the State ! " As the noble Earl, by some brilliant hit, carries the assemblage with a full round of applause, " Ah ! " cries my Yankee friend, with a hearty slap on my shoulder, by Heaven, if he were on our side, we'd make him President—nothing less than President ! "

(LETTERS AND JOURNALS of James, Eighth Earl of Elgin, edited by Theodore Walrond, C. B., 1873. P. 160. (See Appendix Letter G.)

It is not always an easy task to summon, by name, from the mysterious shadowy land, the actors of a distant past, and marshal them instinct with life before succeeding generations; this felicity has befallen us to-night by the discovery of two authentic records, one of 1802, the other of 1835, unexpectedly placed in our hands. The signatures affixed thereto, enable us to reconstruct the little Scottish world of Quebec for both these periods; let us raise a slight corner of the veil!

Several of the bearers of these names, respected professional men or leading merchants, in 1802, are tenderly remembered by their grandsons to this day ; some have left foot-prints " on the sands of time."

The first of these documents is a Memorial to His Majesty George III., signed at Quebec, on the 5th October 1802, by the Rev. Dr. Sparks' congregation and by himself. You are aware that the first Incumbent of St. Andrew's Church—commenced in 1809, and opened for worship on the 30th November 1810—was the Reverend Doctor Alexander Sparks, who had landed at Quebec in 1780, became tutor in the family of Colonel Henry Caldwell at Belmont, St. Foy road, and who died suddenly, in Quebec, on the 7th March, 1819. Dr. Sparks had succeeded to the Rev. George Henry, a military chaplain at the time of the conquest; the first Presbyterian minister, we are told, who officiated in the Province, and who died on the 6th July, 1795, aged 86 years.

One hundred and forty-eight signatures are affixed to this dry-as-dust document of 1802, which we now hold in our hands. It was recently donated to our Society. Strangely indeed, it reads, in 1880.

A carefully prepared petition—it seems—to the King, asking for a site in Quebec whereon to build a church— and suggesting that the lot occupied by the Jesuits' Church, and where until 1878, stood the Upper Town market shambles, be granted to the petitioners, they being without a church, and having to trust to the good will of the Government for the use, on Sundays, of a room in the Jesuits Barracks, as a place of worship.*

Signatures to Memorial addressed to George III, asking for land in Quebec, to build a Presbyterian Church :

Alex. Sparks, Minister;
Jas. Thompson, Jnr.,
Fred. Grant,
Jno. Greenshields,
Chas. G. Stewart,
James Sinclair,
John Urquhart,
William Morrin,
Jno. Eifland,
John Barlie,
Geo. McGregor,
Wm. Holmes,
James Ward,
Jno. Purss,
Ann Watt,
J. Brydon,
Jno. Frazer,
James Somerville,
J. A. Thompson,
Wm. Hall,
Wm. Thompson, Sr.,
D. Monroe,
J. Blackwood,
M. Lymburner,
Francis Hunter,
W. Rouburgh,
John McCord,
J. G. Hanna,
J. McNider,
Adam Lymburner,
Jno. Lynd,
Peter Stuart,
William Grant.
J. A. Todd,
John Mure,

John McLeod,
Hugh Munro,
Geo. Geddes,
Archd. Donaldson,
Sanford Hoyt,
Robert Haddan, Sr.,
Robert Hadden Jr.,
Alex. Hadden,
William Brown,
Geo. Morrison,
Jno. Goudie,
G. Sinclair,
Walter Carruthers,
Wm. Petrie,
John Ross,
Wm. McKenzie,
Thos. Saul,
J. Ross, Jr.,
Ann Ross,
James Mitchell,
Geo. King,
Alex. Thompson,
James Orkney,
J. Neilson,
Daniel Fraser,
A. Ferguson,
Robert Eglison,
Robt. Cairns,
William A. Thompson,
Wm. McWhirter,
John McDonald,
John Auld,
Bridget Young,
Jno. Shaw,
Charles Hunter,

Wm. Anderson,
Hugh McQuarters, Jr.,
W. Norris,
John McClure,
Hugh McQuarters,
Alex. Gibney, Sr.,
Jas Gibney,
Thos. Ewing,
John Glass,
James Tulloch,
Samuel Brown,
Isaac Johnstone,
Peter Leitch
Henry Baldwin,
Daniel Forbes,
William Jaffray,
J. Hendry,
John Thompson,
George Smith,
Wm. Reed,
Alexander Harper,
Robert Marshall,
William White,
Thomas White,
John Taylor,
Adam Reid,
James Irvine,
John Munro,
Alexander Munn,
Alexander Rea,
James Elmslie,
Charles Smith,
Ebenezer Baird,
Lawrence Kidd,
James McCallum,

---

* Quebec Past and Present, p. 404.
See Appendix Letter H.

John Patterson	Geo. Black,	John Burn,
John Crawford.	W. G. Hall,	Joanna George,
John Hewison,	J. Gray,	Maya Darling,
David Douglas,	F. Leslie,	William Lindsay,
George Wilde,	Robt. Wood,	Janet Smith,
Fred. Petry,	Lewis Harper,	William Smith,
James Ross,	Mary Doyle,	Henrietta Sewell,
David Stewart,	A. Anderson,	Jane Sewell,
John Yule,	John Anderson,	C. W. Grant,
Angus McIntyre,	Robt Ross,	Robert Ritchie,
John Mackie,	Wm. Fraser,	George Pyke,
John Purss. Johnston,	Wm. Hay,	Joseph Stilson,
Wm. Thompson, Jr.,	Wm. McKay,	Henry Hunt,
Con Adamson,	Robt. Harrower,	George Thompson.

Quebec, 5th October, 1802.

Some of these signatures are quite suggestive, and will
add materially to the Autograph Album of the Society.
The most notable is probably that of old Adam Lymburner, the cleverest of the three Lymburners, all merchants at Quebec in 1775.* Adam, according to the historian Garneau, was more distinguished for his forensic
abilities and knowledge of constitutional law than for his
robust allegiance to the Hanoverian succession at Quebec,
when Colonel Benedict Arnold and his New Englanders
so rudely knocked at our gates for admission in 1775.

According to Garneau and other historians, in the
autumn of that memorable year, when the fate of British
Canada hung as if by a thread, Adam Lymburner, more
prudent than loyal, retired from the sorely beset fortress
to Charlesbourg, possibly to Château Bigot, a shooting
box then known as the "Hermitage," to meditate on the
mutability of human affairs. Later on, however, in the
exciting times of 1791, Adam Lymburner was deputed by
the colony to England to suggest amendments to the

---

* Adam, the oldest ; John lost at sea on his voyage to England, in the fall
of 1775 ; and Matthew, who, later on, we think was a partner in the old firm
of Lymburner & Crawford, came to his end, in a melancholy manner, at the
Falls of Montmorency, about 1823. Were they all brothers ? we cannot say.
Adam and John were.

project of the constitution to be promulgated by the home authorities. His able speech may be met with in the pages of the *Canadian Review*, published at Montreal, in 1826. This St. Peter street magnate attained four score and ten years, and died at Russell Square, London, on the 10th January, 1836.

Another signature recalls days of strife and alarm ; that of sturdy old Hugh McQuarters, the brave artillery sergeant who, at *Près-de-Ville* on that momentous 31st December 1775, applied the match to the cannon which consigned to a snowy shroud Brigadier-General Richard Montgomery, his two *aides*, McPherson and Cheeseman, and his brave but doomed followers some eleven in all; the rest having sought safety in flight. By this record, it appears Sergeant McQuarters had also a son in 1802 one of Dr. Sparks' congregation. Old Hugh McQuarters lived in Champlain street and closed his career there, in 1812.

Another autograph, that of James Thompson, one of Wolfe's comrades—"a big giant," as our old friend, the late Judge Henry Black who knew him well used to style him, awakens many memories of the past. Sergeant James Thompson, of Fraser's Highlanders, at Louisbourg in 1758, and at Quebec, in 1759, came from Tain, Scotland to Canada as a volunteer to accompany a friend—Capt. David Baillie of the 78th. His athletic frame, courage, integrity and intelligence, during the seventy-two years of his Canadian career, brought him employment, honor, trust and attention from every Governor of the colony from 1759 to 1830, the period of his death ; he was then aged 98 years. At the battle of the Plains of Abraham, James Thompson, as hospital sergeant, was intrusted with the landing at Pointe Lévis of the wounded, who were crossed over in boats ; he tells us of his carrying some of the wounded from the crossing at Levis, up the hill, all the way to the church at St. Joseph converted into an hospital and distant three miles from the present ferry : a six foot giant alone could have been equal to such a task. In 1775, Sergeant Thompson, as overseer of Government works, was charged with erecting the palisades, fascines and other primitive contrivances to keep out Brother Jonathan, who had not yet learned the use of Parrot or Gatling guns, and torpedoes. Later on, we find the sturdy Highlander a subject of curiosity to strangers visiting Quebec—full of siege anecdotes and reminiscences—a welcome guest at the Château in the days of the Earl of Dalhousie. In 1827, as senior Mason, he was called on by His Excellency to give the three magic taps with the hammer, when the corner stone of the Wolfe and Montcalm monument was laid, in the presence of Captain Young of the 79th Highlanders, and a great concourse of citizens. About New Year's day, 1776, Mr. Thompson became possessed of Gen. Montgomery's sword ; it has since passed to his grandson, James Thompson Harrower, whom I see here present, and to whose kindness we are indebted for exhibiting it to you to-night. You will also, no doubt, learn with pleasure that the Society has become possessed of the Thompson M.S.S. letters and papers. Mr. James Thompson left several sons, some of whose signatures are affixed to the document before us. John Gawler was Judge for the District of Gaspé from 1828 to 1865 ; George received a commission in the Royal Artillery ; a third was Deputy Commissary General James Thompson, who died in this city in 1869, and whom many can recall.

Old James Thompson expired in 1830, at the family mansion, St. Ursule Street, now occupied by his grandson, Mr. James Thompson Harrower.

When we name John Greenshields, D. Munro (the partner of the Hon. Matthew Bell) J. Blackwood, Matthew Lymburner, Peter Stuart, William Grant, John Mure, John McNider, J. G. Hanna, John Crawford, David Stewart, (the David Stewart of "Astoria" described by Washing-

ton Irving ?) James Orkney, Robert Wood, Alexander
Munn, James McCallum, Thomas White, Fred. Petrie,
Robert Ritchie, we recall many leading merchants in St.
Peter, Notre-Dame Street and the old *Cul-de-Sac.*

" Jane Sewell," was the wife of Stephen Sewell Solicitor-
General of Lower Canada, brother to Chief Justice Sewell.
" Henrietta Sewell," one of the signers, survived ten years
her husband, the late Jonathan Sewell.* Chief Justice for
Lower Canada, who died in Quebec, in 1839. Chief
Justice Sewell left a numerous progeny : †

" Ebenezer Baird," we take to have been the progenitor
of a well-remembered Quebec Barrister, James E. Baird,
Esq., the *patron* of our city member, Jacques Malouin,
Esquire.

George Pyke, a Halifax Barrister, had settled here.
Subsequently he rose to the Bench as Mr. Justice Pyke.
Robert Harrower was doubtless the father of Messrs.
Robert, David and Charles Harrower, of Trois Saumons,
County of L'Islet. Honorable James Irvine, in 1818, a
member of the Legislative Council was the grandfather of
the Hon. George Irvine, of this city. The Hon. John Jones
Ross, the present Speaker of the Legislative Council,
Quebec, traces back to the " James Ross " of 1802, and the

---

* See Appendix Letter I.

† John Sewell, Capt. in 49th (Brock's Regiment) and Lt.-Col. Volunteers in 1837.
William Smith Sewell, late Sheriff of Quebec, died 1st June, 1866.
Edmund Willoughby Sewell, Clerk in Holy Orders.
Robert Shore Milnes Sewell, Advocate, died 9th May, 1834.
Maria May Livingstone Sewell widow of Major Henry Temple 15th Regiment.
Henrietta Sewell, wife of Rev. Dr. Frs. J. Lundy, died 17th Nov., 1847.
Henry Doyle Sewell, Clerk in Holy Orders.
James Arthur Sewell, M.D., Professor of Laval University.
Montague Charles Sewell, died 28th February, 1859.
Charlotte De Quincy Sewell, died 31st December, 1826.
Fanny Georgina Sewell, wife of Capt. Trevor Davenport, 1st " Royals."
Eliza Janet Sewell, wife of John Ross, Esq., died 8th May, 1875.
Algernon Robinson Sewell, Lt.-Col. 15th Regiment, died 10th January, 1875.

Hon. David Alex. Ross claims for his sire, that sturdy Volunteer of 1759, under Wolfe, "John Ross," who made a little fortune ; he resided at the house he purchased in 1765 near Palace Gate within. He held a Commission as a Captain in the British Militia in 1775, under Colonel Le Maître ; we can recollect his scarlet uniform which he wore in 1775, also worn in 1875, by his grandson, our worthy friend, Hon. D. A. Ross, at the Ball of the Centenary of the repulse of Brigadier General Richard Montgomery, 31st December, 1775. He had three sons, David was Solicitor-General at Montreal, John was a lawyer also, and Prothonotary at Quebec, (the signer of the memorial of 1802), the third died young; of three daughters, one was married to the Rev. Doctor Sparks, already mentioned ; a second was married to Mr. James Mitchell, Deputy A.C.G., and the third to an army surgeon. John Ross, Sr., died at an advanced age. Charles Grey Stewart, our Comptroller of Customs, died in 1854; he was the father of Messrs. McLean, Charles, Alexander, Robert and John Stewart, of Mrs. William Price, of Mrs. William Phillips, of the Misses Ann and Eleanor Stewart.

"Joanna George" the mother of an aged contemporary, Miss Elizabeth George and of * Miss Agnes George, the widow of the late Arch. Campbell, Esq., N.P., and grandmother of the present President of the St. Andrew's Society, W. Darling Campbell, died about 1830.

"Maya Darling" was another daughter, and wife of Capt. Darling. "John Burn," also one of the signers of the Memorial, and who afterwards settled in Upper Canada, was a son of "Joanna George" by another marriage ; the eccentric and clever Quebec Merchant, Mr. James George, was another son. He was the first who sug-

---

* Since the issue of this Lecture, Mrs. Widow Arch. Campbell, closed her long career at Quebec ; in November, 1880, a numerous concourse of friends escorted her remains to that picturesque and last *home* of many Quebecers Mount Hermon Cemetery.

gested, in 1822, the plan of the St. Charles River Docks —the first who took up the subject of rendering the St. Lawrence Rapids navigable higher than Montreal. The idea seemed so impracticable, and what was still worse, so new, that the far-seeing Mr. George, was at the time branded as *non compos !* and still for years the " Spartan," " Passport," " Champion " and other steamers have safely, ran these rapids daily every season !

James George had also suggested the practicability of wooden Railways or Tramways, with horses as locomotive power, forty years before the Civil Engineer Hulburt built the Gosford Wooden Railway, with steam as locomotive power.

" William Grant," of St. Roch's, after whom Grant street was called, was member for the Upper Town of Quebec, during our two first Parliaments, from 17th December 1792, to 29th May 1800, and re-elected 9th January 1805 ; an enterprising and important personage in the little Scotch world of Quebec, was the Honorable Wm. Grant, he had landed in Quebec about 1762 and became an extensive holder of real Estate. When he married the widow of the third Baron de Longueuil in 1771, he was Receiver General of the Province ; his death is recorded in the *Quebec Mercury,* on the 7th October, 1805.

" John Mure " represented the County of York, (Vaudreuil ?) in three Parliaments, from 9th January 1805, to 26th February 1810, and was member for the Upper Town of Quebec from 1810 to 1814. A man of intelligence, he also, though a Presbyterian, became a benefactor to the R. C. Church, having in 1812, given to the parishioners of St. Roch's whereon to erect their church, the site of the R. C. temple of worship, in that thriving suburb.

" John Blackwood," also represented the Upper Town in two Parliaments, from 9th April, 1809, to 20th February, 1810.

"William Lindsay" was the father of the late William Burns Lindsay, for years Clerk of the Legislative Assembly of Lower Canada, and of our venerable fellow citizen Errol Boyd Lindsay Esq., Notary Public, now more than four score years of age ; he seems to have taken his surname from Capt. Errol Boyd, in 1798 commander of the well remembered Quebec and Montreal trader, the "Eureta."

"William Smith" one of the last among the signers of the memorial, the brother of Henrietta Smith wife of Chief Justice Sewell, was the Hon. William Smith, Clerk of the Legislative Council and who in 1815 published his HISTORY OF CANADA in two volumes, a standard work : he was a descendant of the Hon. William Smith, a noted U. E. Loyalist, who wrote the history of the State of New York and landed at Quebec, 23rd October, 1786. As a reward for his loyalty he was made Chief Justice of Lower Canada, 1st September 1785 ; he died at Quebec, 6th December 1793. H. R. H. Prince Edward, followed his remains to the grave.

The names of six signers of the MEMORIAL TO THE KING, appear on the list of the jury impanelled to try, in 1797 before Chief Justice Osgood, David McLane for high treason, viz : John Blackwood, John Crawford, David Munro, John Mure, James Irvine, James Orkney. George Pyke was the Council named *ex officio*, together with M. Franklin, to defend the misguided Yankee.

The Jury stood thus :

John Blackwood.	James Irvine.
John Crawford.	James Orkney.
John Painter.	James Watson Goddard.
David Monro.	Henry Cull.
John Mure.	Robert Morrogh.
John Jones.	George Symes.

The early records of the St. Andrew's Society, founded here in 1835 and kindly submitted for our inspection by

Mr. A. Robertson its Secretary, contain the autographs of many well remembered citizens of Quebec. The first, that of the Manager of the Montreal Bank, Alexander Simpson, who describes himself as "Farmer," of Thornhill,—Thornhill the country seat of our friend, Archibald Campbell, Esquire, P. S. C., eldest son of Col. Chs. Campbell,* of the 99th Regiment.

Mr. Simpson, as Manager of the Bank, had succeeded Mr. Sutherland, for many years Postmaster General of Lower Canada.

This roll of Scotch worthies reminds us each year of the recurrence of the annual dinner in November and of sundry "beef and greens" and "haggis" entertainments given by jolly curlers, the promoters of the "roaring game."

History has even handed down a glowing account of the St. Andrew's dinner, in the stormy days of 1837, given at Schluep's in St. Louis Street the *Globe* Hotel, since, the St. Louis Hotel. It was presided over by that eminent patriot and jurist, the late Andrew Stuart, the father of the present Mr. Justice Andrew Stuart; the Hon. Francis Ward Primrose, for years a leading member of our Bar, was the Vice-President, when the bard and seer of the society, our well remembered old friend, the late Archibald Campbell, usually styled "Her Majesty's Notary," in a clear and mellow voice, poured forth the stirring words of the patriotic lines he had himself composed.

ORIGINAL SONG,

As sung by Archibald Campbell, Esq., at St. Andrew's Dinner, 1837.
AIR : "*Scots wha Hae,*"

Men of Scotia's blood or land,	By gallant hearts those rights were
No longer let us idly stand,	gain'd,
Our "origin" while traitors brand	By gallant hearts shall be maintain'd,
As "foreign" here.	E'en tho' our dearest blood be drain'd
	Those rights to keep.

---

* See Appendix Letter J.

On the crest of Abram's heights,
Victorious in a thousand fights,
The Scottish broad-sword won our
    rights
      Wi' fatal sweep.

Then when the Gaul shall ask again,
Who called us here across the Main ?
Each Scot shall answer, bold and plain,
    " Wolfe sent me here ! "

    Be men like those the hero brought.
    With their best blood the land was bought ;
    And fighting as your fathers fought,
      Keep it or die !

A Saint Andrew's dinner here brings to mind the famous National Banquet, at Halifax, in 1814, at which the sturdy Haligonian Scots sat out, *mirabile dictu,* fifty-two toasts. Some of these toasts were very apposite, others sound strangely to us, after a lapse of sixty-six years.

We subjoin some of the most singular healths drank : to understand the pith of which, one has to recall the warlike era of 1814.

11th. To Alexander, the Emperor of the Russians ....
12th.   " the Emperor of Austria...............................
13th.   " the King of Prussia......................................
14th.   " Louis XVIII. May he recollect the nation which afforded him protection during the unprecedented trouble of his country, and was the chief cause in restoring him to the throne of France, Air—" The White Cockade."
15th.   " Congress of Vienna ....
22nd.   " British Commissioners at Ghent ....
26th.   A rather humorous one. " May James Madison and all his faction be soon compelled to resign the reins of Government in America, and seek a peace establishment with their friend Bonaparte at Elba." Airs— "The Rogue's March" and " Go to the Devil and shake yourself." (Such sentiments have long since passed away.)
29th. To General Count Platoff and his brave Cossacks. Air— "The Cossack."
31st.   " the gallant Veteran Blucher.
36th.   " the memory of General Moreau.
40th.   "   "   " of Prince Kutusoff and all those who have fallen in the defence of the liberties of Europe.

43rd.   Typifies commerce—"Horn, Corn, Fish and Yarn —"Reel of Tullochgorum."

48th.   " Robert Gibb's contract, "Johnny Grey's Breeks." (Some good hit made here no doubt sixty-six years ago.)

50th.   " the Beggar's Benison. Air—"The Rogue's March."

51st.   May Great Britain never resign the right of search while she has a sailor or a soldier to defend "it." (This toast would cause a smile at the present day.)*

THE QUEBEC CURLING CLUB—1838.

" The annual match between the married men and bachelors of the Quebec Curling Club was played on the 1st of March, for " beef and greens," when the following was the result of the game:

Married men, 17; Bachelors, 31.

The following gentlemen were players:

Married men—Messrs. R. H. Gairdner, William Patton, L. T. McPherson, William Phillips and John Dyde. Bachelors—Messrs. James Gillespie, John P. Anderson, George Gillespie, James Burns and Thomas Hamilton.

The dinner of " beef and greens " with some other good things, took place on Saturday last, at the *Globe*. Several guests were invited to partake of the hospitality of the Club, and the evening was spent in a very pleasant manner."†

The portly President of the Society, Andrew Paterson, and his Board of Officers are all too well remembered for us to do more than inscribe here their names, in order to show how the Scotch element stood in Quebec forty-five years ago. What could we tell you which you do not already know, about those dear friends and relatives of so many present here this evening? To our youthful eyes in 1838, none, however, appeared so imposing as Captain Rayside when he marched from the Barracks, the Queen's Stores Champlain Street, his corps of Volunteer Seamen, the QUEEN'S PETS, habited in pea jackets, and trailing formidable cutlasses, whilst the Volunteer Band rejoiced in a swarthy Ethiopian in charge of the big drum.

---

* *Antiquarian* for Oct., 1880, p. 67.

† *Quebec Gazette*, 12 March, 1838.

The Society was formed in October 1835, and the notices for the first meeting ran as follows:—

Persons friendly to the formation of a Society, to be called "The Quebec St. Andrew's Society," are requested to meet at the Albion Hotel, on Friday next, the 9th instant, at 3 o'clock, P.M.

Andrew Paterson,	David Burnet,	James Gibb,
A. Simpson,	John Strang,	Ronald McLellan,
A. H. Young,	John Fisher,	James Burns,
John Bruce,	John Neilson,	George Black,
Jas. Denholm,	Allan Gilmour,	John Thompson,
D. Wilkie,	Donald Fraser,	J. Douglas.
Jos. Morrin,	Charles Stuart,	

Quebec, 3rd October, 1835.

MEETING AT THE ALBION HOTEL, FRIDAY, 9TH OCTOBER, 1835.

PRESENT:

Hon. John Stewart,	Thomas Elder,	R. H. Gairdner.
Andrew Paterson,	R. MacDonald,	John Fife,
John Neilson,	J. B. Edie,	L. J. McNair.
W. McTavish,	D. Burnet,	D. Fraser,
P. Moir,	J. Thompson,	W. K. Rayside,
A. Laurie,	R. MacLellan,	A. Simpson,
C. Bruce,	L. Ballingall,	J. Bruce,
A. McGill,	T. A. Young,	D. Wilkie,
A. Gilmour,	Jas. Burns,	James Dean,
John Young,		

Andrew Paterson in the Chair.

Moved by A. Simpson, seconded by A. Gilmour,—"That it is expedient to form a Society in this city, to be called the Saint Andrew's Society of Quebec."

ELECTION OF OFFICERS FOR YEAR ENDING 30TH NOV., 1836.

Andrew Paterson...... ....President.
John Neilson........................ 1st Vice-President.
The Hon. John Stewart.........2nd Vice-President.

MANAGERS:

James Dean, George Black, Donald MacLellan, Allan Gilmour,
Lewis J. McNair, Hon. F. W. Primrose, Samuel Neilson,
Robert Pope Ross, Donald Fraser, Thomas
Ainslie Young.

CHAPLAINS:—Rev. John Clugeston, and Rev. Daniel Wilkie.

PHYSICIANS:—Joseph Morrin, James Douglas.

Alex. Simpson, Treasurer. | John Bruce, Secretary,
Jas. Gillespie, Asst.-Secretary.

COMMITTEE OF INSTALMENT:

William McTavish, | Robert H. Gairdner.

OFFICERS OF ST. ANDREW'S SOCIETY FOR 1880.

PRESIDENT—W. D. Campbell. FIRST VICE-PRESIDENT—Wm. Rae.
SECOND VICE-PRESIDENT—D. R. McLeod.

TREASURER—Jas. McNider. SECRETARY—A. Robertson.

COMMITTEE OF MANAGEMENT—Messrs. Wm. Brodie, D. H. George,
P. Johnston, Wm. Sutherland and D. Kerr.

CHAPLAINS—Rev. Dr. Cook and Rev. W. B. Clark.

PHYSICIAN—Dr. Rowand.

Out of the population of the City of Quebec—per
census of 1871... 59,699
The Scotch element stands thus 1,861

The Quebec Press owes its orgin to two Scotchmen,
from Philadelphia, Messrs. Brown & Gilmore, who printed* on the 21st June, 1764, in this city, the first number
of the *Quebec Gazette*, the oldest paper in the Province,
the Montreal *Gazette* having been founded fourteen years
later by Fleury Mesplet, in 1778. When the *Gazette* was
bought up in 1864, and merged into the *Quebec Morning
Chorniele*, founded in 1847, it had existed 110 years.

William Brown was succeeded in the editorship and
proprietorship of this venerable sheet, by his nephew
Samuel Neilson, the elder brother of John Neilson, who
for years was the trusted Member for the County of

---

* The handle or lever of this press I now hold in my hand.

Quebec; as widely known as a Journalist, a Legislator and in 1822, oui worthy Ambassador to England—as he was respected as a patriot.

Samuel Neilson had died in 1793;—his young brother and *protegé*, John, born at Dornald in Scotland, in 1776, being in 1794 a minor, the *Gazette* was conducted by the late Rev. Dr. Alex. Sparks his guardian until 1796. When John Neilson became of full age, he assumed the direction of the paper for more than half a century, either in his name or in that of his son Samuel. Hon. John Neilson, closed his long and spotless career, at his country seat (Dornald) at Cap Rouge, on the 1st February 1848, aged 71 years. Who has not heard of the Nestor of the Canadian Press, honest John Neilson ? May his memory ever remain bright and fragrant—a beacon to guide those treading the intricate paths of journalism—a shining light to generations yet unborn !

In a pretty rustic cemetery, the site of which was presented by himself to the Presbyterian Church of Valcartier, near Quebec, were laid, on the 4th February, 1848, the remains of this patriotic man—escorted by citizens of every origin, after an eloquent address had been delivered by the Rev. Dr. John Cook, the present pastor of St. Andrew's Chnrch.

We are indebted to his son John Neilson, Esq., of Dornald, for this relic, the iron lever of the first Press used at Quebec in 1764—a precious one to Canadian journalism.

There are indeed many Scotch names associated with our press. Space precludes us from enlarging more on this subject. We cannot, however, close this portion of our enquiry, without naming Daniel Wilkie, LL.D., the editor of the Quebec *Star*,—a literary gazette founded in 1818—still better remembered as the esteemed instructor of Quebec youth for forty years.

Dr. Wilkie was born at Tollcross, in Scotland, in 1777,

one year later than John Neilson ; he settled in Quebec in 1803, and died here on the 10th May, 1851.

Among those present this evening, I see some of his former pupils. Alas ! the frost of years has silvered their locks ! Dr. Wilkie " broke the bread of science" to several youths, who subsequently won honor among their fellow men. Among the illustrious dead, might be recalled (in the days when the able member for Birmingham, England, John Arthur Roebuck was indentured, at Quebec in 1818, as law student, to Thos. Gugy, Esq., Barrister, brother of Col. B. C. A. Gugy, late of Darnoc, Beauport,) a favorite pupil of the Doctor, the late Hon. Judge Hy. Black, as well as that eminent jurist and scholar, Alex. C. Buchanan, Q.C., late of Montreal ; Hon. Mr. Justice T. C. Aylwin, Judge Chs. Gates Holt. Among those still moving in our midst, one likes to point to Chief Justice Duval, Judges Andrew Stuart, George Okill Stuart, and Hon. J. Chapais, Hon. David A. Ross, Messrs. Francis and Henry Austin, Daniel McPherson, N.P., R. H. Russel, M.D., and John Russel, of Toronto, M.D.

Dr. Wilkie's pupils had the following truthful words inscribed, on the monument they erected to their patron in Mount Hermon cemetery ;

" He was a learned scholar
And indefatigable student of philosophy and letters
An able and successful instructor of youth,
Of genuine uprightness and guileless simplicity
A devout, benevolent and public spirited man."

Some Scotch names are still remembered in Montreal journalism, such as that of Robert Weir—of David Kinnear—of James Moir Ferres.

Not many years back, the editorial pen of our leading Journal, the *Morning Chronicle*, was held by a Scotch writer of distinction Daniel C. Morrison ; a cultured Scotchman, George Stewart, Jr., wields it still—the able historian of Lord Dufferin's administration. May that upright spirit, that proud regard for duty, infused into our press by such master-minds as John Neilson and Daniel Wilkie, still continue to inspire the "Fourth Estate," whether confided to Scotch or other hands.

Ladies and Gentlemen, we have uttered the word "education" in connection with the Scotch element in the Province of Quebec and space commands us to be brief. Rest assured that the love of instruction, which has in the past so powerfully helped to mould the popular mind north of the Tweed, and has found a vent in the Scotch parochial school system, had also its votaries on our shores.

Who has not heard of the liberal endowments made by Scotchmen, in our commercial metropolis, Montreal ? of fortunes spent in founding seats of learning or building up that proud city ? fortunes accumulated in Montreal or in those great trading companies of the Hudson Bay and the lone land of the North. Scotch capital and enterprise formed colonies and settlements in these Northern latitudes, such as Selkirk's. Lord Selkirk was ably seconded by another Scotchman knighted for his services and public spirit, Sir George Simpson, who died in Montreal, in 1860. Monuments most creditable to the cause of education were erected by them also. Who has not heard of the McTavishes, McGillivrays, McLeods, McKenzies, McGills, McLaughlins and their successors, as discoverers, merchants, travellers, barons in the bank parlor, patrons of education. That noble seat of learning in Montreal, the University of McGill College—who imparted to it the breath of life ? a Scotchman, the Hon. James McGill ! * Who again was one of its truest friends and most useful Presidents ? another Scotchman, the Hon Peter McGill ! who in September last, so munificently endowed its Museum ?

---

* Born at Glasgow in 1744, a successful merchant, a member of Parliament, subsequently, a member of the Legislative Council ; finally, an Executive Councillor, he served in the war of 1812, when he became a Brigadier-General-

a Scot, Mr. Redpath!—men distinguished, for their bene-
factions, wealth and intelligence. If you should long for
more proof of the feelings of Scotchmen towards mental
culture and education ; Look round! Reflect on the spot
where you stand ! To whom does Quebec owe this roof
which shelters us to night, the Morrin College ! To the
thoughtful munificence of a Scotchman, Dr. Joseph Morrin.
Honor to his name. (*Loud applause.*)

On every side we look, some memento recalls for Scotia's
sons, a glorious past. Before you, there, stands the quaint
model of the first steamship which crossed with steam the
Atlantic : the "Royal William," manned by a Scot, Capt.
John MacDougall. A Scot, at Quëbec, in 1831, George
Black, laid her keel in the shipyard, at *Ance des Mères*,
owned by Messrs. Sheppard & Campbell.

To whom does the Literary and Historical Society owe
its origin ? To a progressive and public spirited Vice-roy
of Canada, George Ramsay, Earl of Dalhousie, a Scotch
nobleman.

Would you like to hear how it originated ? We will
briefly tell you. In the autumn of 1823, His Excellency
the Governor General of Canada assembled round him
the *élite* of Quebec Society and invited their co-operation
to a literary project over which he had long meditated. On
the 6th January 1824, we next find him. surrounded by
the most distinguished citizens of Quebec of all origins,
at the Chateau-Saint Louis yonder, his official residence:
the Sewells, Stuarts, Aylwins, Bayfields, Sheppards, Wick-
steads, Mountains, McCords, McKenzies, Morrins, Wilkies,
Henrys, Blacks, Primroses—join hands with the Valliéres,
the Signaï, the Demers, the Carons, the Garneaus, the Bou-
chettes, the Faribaults, the Taschereaus, the Perraults ; the
Charter of the Society is drafted, with the able assistance
of Dr. John Charlton Fisher, ex-Editor of the New York
Albion, recently settled in Quebec ; and was subsequently
sanctioned by His Majesty, George IV.

It was stated, in the earlier part of this paper, that Scotchmen, in this Province, have made their mark in the marts of commerce, as well as in the loftier regions of thought and statecraft.*

As to the first, the array of names on the Exchange Register is so ample, that it is quite sufficient to mention a few of the best known, such as that of Allan, Edmonstone, Ross, Young, Thomson, McPherson, Gibb, McGill, Redpath, McTavish, Anderson, Dow, Angus, Ferrier, Torrance.

Literary Canada is proud of its Stuarts, Logans, Wilsons, Dawsons, Murdocks, Lyalls,, Campbells, Rattrays, Evan, McCall, Alexander McLaughlin, W. and Alex. Garvie, Robert Murray, and a host of others.

The voice of a Neilson, a Galt, a Robertson, a Ross, an Ogilvie, in our Commons at Quebec, has responded to that of a Morris, a McDougall, a Brown, a McKenzie, a Mac-Donald in the Supreme Council, of the nation, at Ottawa.

Ladies and Gentlemen, I am not here to sing pœans to Scottish success, I stand before you to-night merely to notice the relative position the race occupies, as a notable element in our nationality, in the manner I previously did, with the respect to the descendant of the Gaul.

With such hopeful materials—such energetic factors, as the free, the sturdy Briton—the cultured descendant of the Norman—the self-reliant Scot—the ardent, eloquent Milesian, there exists in those fertile, northern realms ruled over by England's gentle Queen, the component parts of a great commonwealth, which will gradually consolidate, itself with the modifications time may bring, into the national organization, under which Canadians of all creeds and origins, in 1867, associated, in a vast and liberty-loving Confederation. (*Loud and prolonged applause.*)

---

* See Appendix Letter K.

APPENDIX.

[See page 6.]

JACQUES CARTIER'S OFFICERS AND CREW.

Liste de l'Equipage de Jacques Cartier, conservée dans les archives de St. Malo, France—revue avec soin sur le *fac-similé*, par C. H. Laverdière, Ptre., Bibliothécaire de l'Université Laval, 22 novembre 1859.

Jacques Cartier, capne.
Thomas Fourmont, Me. de la nef.
Guille. Le breton Bastille, capne. et pilote du Galion.
Jacq Maingar, me. du Galion.
Marc Jalobert, capne. et pilote du Courlieu,
Guille. Le Marié, me du Courlieu.
Laurent Boulain.
Estienne Nouel.
PIERRE ESMERY DICT TALBOT.
MICHEL HERUÉ.
Estienne Reumevel.
Michel Audiepore.
Bertrand Samboste.
Richard Lebay, Faucamps.
Lucas père Sr. ou Lucas Jacq, Sr., Fammys.
Françoys Guitault, Apoticaire.
Georges Mabille.
Guillme. Sequart, charpentier.
Robin Le Fort.
Sampson Ripault, Barbier.
Françoys Guillot.
Guille. Esnault, charpentier.
Jehan Dabin, charpentier.
Jehan Duuert.
Jullien Golet.
Thomas Boulain.
Michel Philipot.

Eustache Grossin.
Guillme. Allierte.
Jehan Ravy.
Pierres Marquier, trompet.
Guille. Legentilhomme.
Raoullet Maingard.
Françoys Duault.
HERUÉ HENRY.
Yvon Legal.
Anthoine Alierte.
Jehan Colas.
Jacq Poinsault.
Dom Guille. Le Breton.
Dom Antoine.
Philipe Thomas, charpentier.
Jacq. Duboys.
Julien Plantiruet.
Jehan Go.
Jehan Legentilhomme.
Michel Douquais, charpentier.
Jehan Aismery, charpentier.
Pierre Maingart.
Lucas Clauier.
Goulset Riou.
Jehan Jacq de Morbihan.
Pierre Nyel.
Legendre Estienne Leblanc.
Jehan Pierres.
Jehan Commuyres.
Anthoine Desgranches.

Jehan Hamel.
Jehan Fleury.
Guille. Guilbert.
Colas Barbe.
Laurens Gaillot.
Guille. Bochier.
Michel Eon.
Jean Anthoine.
Michel Maingard.
Jehan Margen.
Bertrand Apuril.
Giles Staffin.
Geoffroy Olliuler.
GUILLE DE GUERNEZÉ,

Louys Douayrer.
Pierre Coupeaulx.
Pierres Jonchée.—74 signatures.

The subsequent seven signatures were added in the answer to the Quebec Prize Historical Questions, submitted in 1879.

Jean Gouyon.
Charles Gaillot.
Claude de Pontbrians.
Charles de la Pommeraye.
Jean Poullet.
Philippe Rougemont.
De Goyelle.

B.

[See Page 22.]

CLUNIE MACPHERSON.

Capt. John Macpherson, of Fraser's Highlanders, wounded 25th July, 1759, was brother to Duncan Macpherson, the head of the Clan, the Laird of Cluny, generally known by the name of Clunie Macpherson. The melancholy end of this brave chieftain places in a most favorable light, the fidelity of his followers towards their chiefs mixed up in the rebellion of 1715 and also in the rising of 1745. The battle of Culloden brought ruin on all the Clan. Clunie Macpherson was, however, appointed to a company in Lord Loudon's Highlanders, and had taken the oath to the Government. His Clan was impatient to join the adventurous descendant of their ancient sovereign, when he came to claim what they supposed his right. While he hesitated between duty and inclination, his wife, a daughter of Lord Lovat, and a staunch jacobite, earnestly dissuaded him from breaking his oath, assuring him nothing could end well that began with perjury. His friends reproached her for interfering and hurried on the husband to his ruin."—*Sketches of the Highlanders,* Vol. I, P. 60.

His life was thus forfeited to the laws, and much diligence was exerted to bring him to justice. He lived nine years in a cave, at a short distance from his house, which had been burned to the ground by the King's troops. "This cave, says General Stewart" was in the front of a woody precipice, the trees and shelving rocks completely concealing the entrance. It was dug out by his own people, who worked by night, and conveyed the stones and rubbish into a lake in the neighborhood, that no vestige of their labour might betray the retreat of their master. In this sanctuary he lived secure, occasionally visiting his friends by night, or when time slackened the vigor of the search.

Upwards of a hundred persons knew where he was concealed and a reward of £1,000 was offered to any one who should give information against him; and as it was known that he was concealed on his estate, eighty men were constantly stationed there, besides the parties continually marching into the country to intimidate his tenantry, and induce them to disclose the place of his concealment.

Sir Hector Munro, at that time a Lieutenant in the 34th Regiment, was entrusted with the command of a large party, and continued two whole years in Badenach, for the purpose of discovering Clunie's retreat. The unwearied vigilance of the Clan could alone have saved him from the vigilance of this party, directed as it was by an officer equally remarkable for his zeal, and his knowledge of the country and people. The slightest inattention, even a momentary want of caution or presence of mind on the part of the Macphersons, would infallibly have betrayed his retreat; yet so true were the Clan, so strict in the observance of secrecy and so dexterous in conveying to him unobserved the necessaries he required that although the soldiers were animated with the hope of reward and a step of promotion was promised to the officer who should apprehend him, not a trace of him could be discovered, nor an individual found base enough to give a hint to his detriment. Many anecdotes have been related of the narrow escapes which he made including the vigilance of the soldiery, especially when he ventured to spend a few of the dark hours conversably with his friends; and also of the diligence, fidelity and presence of mind displayed by the people in concealing his retreat, and baffling the activity of his pursuers, during a period of no less than nine years. At length, however, wearied out with this dreary and hopeless state of existence, and taught to despair of pardon, he escaped to France in 1755, and died there the following year. Clunie had become so cautious, whilst leading the life of an outlaw that, on parting with his wife, or his most attached friends, he never told them to which of his places of concealment he was going, nor suffered anyone to accompany him. Not that he had any suspicion of the fidelity of his family, his friends, or his Clan; their attachment and devotion had been too well tried to admit of so unjust and ungrateful a thought entering his mind. His object was that when questioned by his pursuers they might be enabled to answer, that they knew not whither he had gone, or where he lay concealed."

THE KILT WORN BY CHOICE.

[See Page 25.]

"It is extraordinary that there are two Regiments (the 71st and 72nd) the oldest embodied Clan corps, should wear trousers or trews, a dress formerly confined to lame, sick or aged Highlanders. IT HAS BEEN A SOURCE OF GREAT VEXATION TO THEM, THEIR CLAN AND THEIR COUNTRY. Assuredly, Lord McLeod, the eldest son of Mackenzie, Earl of Cromarty, who raised the 73rd, now the

71st, and Mackenzie, Earl of Seaforth, who embodied the old 78th, now the 72nd, would never have thought of AN ALTERATION, SO UNNECESSARY AND SO UNCONGENIAL TO CELTIC FEELING. WHOEVER HAS THE HIGH HONOUR TO COMMAND THE BRITISH ARMY, SHOULD NOT FORGET HOW SRONGLY THE HIGH-MINDED AND BRAVE GAEL, ARE ATTACHED TO THEIR NATIONAL COSTUME; and as these regiments have still the name of Highlanders, and are composed of them, it is to be hoped their appropriate military costume will be yet restored to them."

"While on this subject I cannot avoid noticing an unaccountable practice in some Highland regiments where the officers seldom appear in the feilabeag, except on field days and particular occasions! Is it from an idea that it is unbecoming, or that the privates are only obliged to wear the kilt? It is a strange inconsistency and a very unmilitary custom, for which I presume the respective Colonels or Adjutants are answerable. Having some time since lived four or five years where the 78th Rosshire Buffs were stationed, I MUST EXONERATE THAT CORPS FROM THE ABOVE REFLECTIONS, officers and men being always dressed in proper regimentals.

I know, from my own experience, that all the men being Scotch, all the Scotch officers are deeply attached to the kilt, and would not change it for any other uniform, however splendid—A few English officers, on joining Highland regiments, are apt to ridicule the kilt, and thus foster an idea that the five kilted regiments, do not wear the feilabeag by choice, but I have uniformly observed, that after serving a short time amongst the Highlanders these would-be critics, become the most enthusiastic admirers of the dress.

I have worn the kilt myself as child, boy and man, and maintain that a warmer, a more comfortable dress could not have been invented for the Highlands of Scotland, the tartan being three ply thick round the body, and the feet encased in thick stockings, vital heat is kept in two of the most important parts of the human frame, while the knees after a time become hardened and capable of bearing any exposure. How far the kilt is adapted to the climate of Canada, is not in my province to say, and I believe that the authorities intend ordering the 78th to discontinue the kilt for the winter, but of this I am certain, were a stipulation made to discontinue the dress for good, the Rosshire Buffs would sooner be frozen on their posts than discard forever their national costume.

COLIN MACKENZIE, Capt. 78th Rosshire Buffs.

C.

[See Page 29.]

HON. JAMES LESLIE.

(1786-1873.)

"Another veteran has been removed from the political arena. The Hon. James Leslie, Senator, whose death is reported from Montreal, has at one time played a conspicuous part in the affairs of the country, though of late years he had been content to rest on his laurels. He was the son of Capt. James Leslie, 15th Regiment, who was Assistant-Quarter-Master to the army of General Wolfe at the capture of Quebec, and who claimed descent from a junior branch of the family of Rothes, and on his mother's side from John Stuart, of Inchbreck in the Mearns, lineally descended from Murdock, Duke of Albany. The subject of the present notice was born at Kair, Kincardine, on the 4th September, 1786, and was educated at the Aberdeen Grammar School, and afterwards at Marischal College and Aberdeen University. He married, in 1815, a daughter of Patrick Langan, Seigneur of Bourchemin and De Ramsay, formerly an officer in the British army. Mr. Leslie was for many years an extensive merchant in Montreal. He served in the Volunteers in the war of 1812, and retired from the Militia many years afterwards with the rank of Lieutenant-Colonel. He was a member of the Executive Council of Canada and President of that body from March to September, 1848; and Provincial Secretary and Registrar from 1848 to October, 1851. He sat as a representative from Montreal, in the Lower Canada Assembly, from 1824 until the Union of that province with Upper Canada in 1840. He represented Verchères in the Assembly of Canada from 1841 to March, 1848, when he was summoned to the Legislative Council, of which he remained a member until the Confederation, in 1867. He had been an unsuccessful candidate for the county of Montreal at the general elections of 1841. He was appointed a Senator by Royal Proclamation in 1867, and remained a member of that body until his death, which took place at the advanced age of eighty-seven in 1873. Mr. Leslie had always acted with the Conservatives."

D.

[See Page 31.]

The following ancedote, taken from the "*Letters of a Volunteer,*" communicated by Capt. Colin Mackenzie, appears worthy of being remembered:

"On board of the STERLING CASTLE, in the River St. Lawrence,
two miles below Quebec,
Sept. 2, 1759.

"Notwithstanding the check we receeived in the action (at Beauport), of the 31st of July, it must be admitted our people behaved with great vivacity. I cannot omit being particular with respect to a singular instance of personal bravery and real courage.

Captain Ochterlony and Lieutenant Peyton (both of General Moncton's regiment) were wounded, and fell before the breast-work near the Falls.—The former, mortally, being shot through the body; the latter was wounded only in the knee. Two savages pushed down upon them with the utmost precipitation, armed with nothing but their diabolical knives. The first seized on Captain Ochterlony, when Mr. Peyton, who lay reclining on his fusee, discharged it; the savage dropt immediately on the body of his intended prey.

The other savage advanced with much eagerness to Mr. Peyton, who had no more than time to disengage his bayonet, and conceal its disposition— with one arm he warded off the purposed blow, and with the other stung him to the heart; nevertheless, the savage, tho' fallen, renewed his attempts, insomuch that Mr. Peyton was obliged to repeat his blow, and stab him through and through the body.

A straggling grenadier, who had happily escaped the slaughter of his companions, stumbled upon Captain Ochterlony and readily offered him his services. The Captain, with the spirit and bravery of a true Briton, replied, "Friend, I thank you,—but with respect to me, the musquet, or scalping knife, will be only a more speedy deliverance from pain—I have but a few minutes to live. Go—make haste—and tender your services where there is a possibility they may be useful."—At the same time he pointed to Mr. Peyton, who was then endeavouring to crawl away on the sand.

The grenadier took Mr. Peyton on his back, and conveyed him to the boat, but not without each receiving a wound—Mr. Peyton in his back and his rescuer, another near his shoulder."

E

Letter from Brigadier-General the Hon. James Murray, son of Alexander, fourth Lord Elibank, to his brother, Rear-Admiral the Hon. George Murray.

(Communicated to the Literary and Historical Society of Quebec, by Capt. Colin McKenzie, 78th Highlanders, R. B., an Associate Member of the Society.)

Quebec, October, the 11th, 1759.

" MY DEAR BROTHER,

The news of the battle of Quebec will have reached you long before this can come to your hands. I had too great a share in it to condescend to particulars; because I hold it odious to speak of one's self. I have the honor to be appointed Governor of Quebec and the conquer'd country, which is a noble one indeed,—infinitely beyond what any Britain imagin'd it to be, whether for the fertility of its soil, or number of its inhabitants. I have now serv'd two campaigns under three officers who were put over my head, and I don't find I have got a regiment yet, tho' I have had the strongest assurances from the Ministers. I think I cannot miss it now, and I believe my enemys will agree that I have earn'd it. I enjoy great health in America; the cruel disorder in my stomach is entirely cured. It was certainly nervous, and the severity of the Nova Scotia frost braced me up, and has made me the strongest man in the army.

* * * * * * * * * * * * *

I have taken it into my head you will hear good news from me in the spring. I am making provision of snow-shows for a winter expedition and will not allow the Chevalier de Levi to be quiet in his cantonments. I have an eye to his magazines. I have six thousand as brave troops as ever existed. Business may and shall be done with them, that those who have hitherto deprived me of my preferement may repine at it. Your old acquaintance Saunders is much my friend. He is a worthy brave fellow ; and if it lys in your way, I wish you would wait upon him, and let him know how much I think myself obliged to him. Make my compliments to all my relations about you, and be assured that I am sincerely yours,"

JAMES MURRAY.

(The old orthography has been retained in both letters]

FROM THE SAME TO THE SAME.

Quebec, October 19th, 1760.

" MY DEAR GEORGE,

Yours of the 12th July did not come to hand till yesterday. Your son Patrick, I told you before, I should take off your hands. The commission is not yet made out for him, but it is settled he is to have it. It would now have been done, had I known his christian name, when I was in Montreal.

*   *   *   *   *   *   *   *   *   *   *   *   *   *

You seem to be nettled at the silence of the newswriters; but if you'll coolly consider I am highly honored thereby. Mr. Townshend, Monkton, &c., &c., &c., were in the right, perhaps, to hire these miscreants to relate feates they never performed, and to ascribe to themselves the actions of other men. I don't want such false trappings ; it is the praise of my brother soldiers I am ambitious of, and I flatter myself I have their esteem. I have the satisfaction to know that my conduct has the approbation of his Majesty and his Ministers. I have served my country with an honest, hearty zeal, and shall continue to exert the poor faculties I have, in any station I may be placed in. A steady adherance to these principals will succeed in the end ; and get the better of all sculkers, jack-daws, and gazateers. It will no doubt be known hereafter to all the world, who opposed the attack of the lines at Montmorency, and who in the beginning, and to the very last of the campaign, urged the descent above the town at the very place where it was made. And surely no body is ignorant of what the left wing of the army did the day of the 13th of September ; it was not *en potence :* it broke the enemy's line, and pursued the fugitives to the gates, and would have compleated their destruction, had it not been called off by superior authority. It must be allow'd that to maintain the conquest in the situation I was left in, was a much more arduous task than the acquisition of it ; that was the business of two or three hours, in which fortune was most partial to us ; the other was a series of toils, alarms, intrigues, finesses, and, in short, of everything that is comprehended in war. My journal in the hands of the Minister points out all at large. You shall see it when we meet; and you will allow that Monkton and Townshend gave up a field of glory when they abandon'd Quebec, which they can never recover, were they to keep in constant pay all the scriblers under the sun. I fought a battle : I lost it. What then ? Is every day of battle a day of victory ? Did it be asked any soldier if, in my situation, it was right to fight. He will answer without hesitation, "To be sure." Examine the disposition, compare it with the ground which must determine the propriety of it, and I fl tter myself it will be allow'd a good one. Was not the critical moment of attack made use of ? Did it succeed ? Was not the victory gain'd, had the right wing been as active and as vigorous the 28th of April, 1760, as the left was the 13th of September, 1759 ? Was not aid instantly given during the action where it was wanted ? Were not the cannon judiciously placed ? Does not all this denote a presence of mind, and a *coup d'oile ?* Where was the General in this battle—Betwixt his own line and that of the enemy—everywhere, where the enemy made a push, animating his men by his presence. He had two horses shot under him, and his clothes riddled by the enemy's musketry. Where was he when the right wing faulter'd ? He was placing the cannon on the hights, in the centre, but rode instantly to the right, and there recover'd the confusion. How did the troops retreat into town ? In tolerable order by the means of the corps the General himself posted in the two unfinished redoubts, and on an eminence. Did he stay with the corps himself to the last ? He did, he was the last man that enter'd the gates. The defence of the place, as it was successful, in England (where everything is right or wrong agreeable to the decision of Dame Fortune) will answer for its self. You are to ask the French Generals what share had this campaign in the total reduction of Canada. I am persuaded Mr. Amherst is too just to be silent on that head. He certainly has told that I left him nothing to do, and that the Marquis de Vaudreuil insinuated terms of surrender to me, before Mr. Amherst's army appear'd, which I would not listen to, as I had intelligence of the commander-in-chief's being within six days' march of me, and I was posted at Longviel, by which the junction of the three armys was infallible.

This much I have open'd myself to my brother ; it is very wrong for a man to speak of himself, but he that praises himself is unpardonable. I therefore conjure you not to show this letter to any body but Elibank ; he and you may make what use of the contents you please, provided you do not let it be known that I have trumpeted my own fame.

I think myself accountable to my family in a very particular manner for my actions, especially as the sphere I have lately acted in has been eminent. It will be your business to dive into the truth of every sentence of this letter, but not to expose me to the reproach of vain glory. I offer my very affectionate compliments to all my relations round you, and am, my Dear George.

Your most affectionate brother and sincere friend,

JAMES MURRAY.

Sandy Johnstone now lives with me, and acts as my Brigade-Major. He is very fat, but we have nothing to do.

Brig.-General Murray's "*Journal*" was published under the auspices of the Literary and Historical Society in 1871.

REMARKS.

These two valedictory letters of General Murray addressed to his brother Admiral Murray, appeared, with other corespondence, in the History of the Earls of Cromarty, compiled by Mr William Fraser, F. S. A. Scot, and issued privately last year by the Duke and Duchess of Sutherland. Admiral Murray afterwards succeeded his elder brother Patrick, and became sixth Lord Elibank. He married Lady Isabella Mackenzie, daughter of George third and last Earl of Cromarty ; their daughter, the Hon. Maria Murray, married Mr. Hay, of Newhall, (brother of the seventh Marquis of Tweedale), and succeeding to the Cromarty-Mackenzie estates on the death of her cousin, Kenneth Mackenzie, took the name of Hay-Mackenzie, and was the grandmother of the present Duchess of Sutherland, who, in 1861, was created Countess of Cromarty in her own right. This, therefore, explains how General Murray's letters found their way into the Cromarty charter chest.

The letters are, I think, of considerable interest. In the first, written only a month after the battle of the Plains of Abraham, General Murray announces to his brother that he has been appointed Governor of Quebec, he also states that he is at the head of 6,000 trained troops, and that he contemplates a winter expedition against the Chevalier de Levis, and especially has an eye to his magazines. The Chevalier, who was cantoned at Fort Jacques-Cartier, had formed the design of attacking the City as soon as the river should be ice-bound, and when Murray could expect no assistance from the English fleet. The French General was obliged to retreat on Montreal. In the meantime, Murray vigorously pushed forward the repairs of the fortifications of Quebec, but the insufficiency and badness of provisions and the rigour of the climate introduced scurvy and other complaints among the troops, and had reduced his garrison to about one-half, when, on the 26th April, 1760, he heard that the Chevalier de Levis, having collected about 10,000 men, had landed at Pointe-aux-Trembles.

We may now turn to the second letter. It was written a year after the first, and six months after the events I am about to summarize. The General commences by stating that it is only the approbation of his Sovereign the Ministers and his brother soldiers that he is desirous of obtaining, and after referring to his share in the battle of the Plains of Abraham, he proceeds to defend the action he took on the day of the 28th of April.

As soon as he heard that De Levis had landed, Murray advanced to Sillery, and there determined to give him battle. He says in his letter : " My " journal in the hands of the Minister points out all at large." Reviewing Murray's conduct, General Sir E. Cust, in his " Wars of the eighteenth century," says : " Murray now resolved on a plan which has been much criticised " and justly condemned. He thus explained his view of the case, in his dis- " patch to the Secretary of State—that the enemy was greatly his superior in " numbers, but considering that the British forces were habituated to victory, " and were provided with a fine train of artillery, he thought that an action in " the field was less risk in the single chance of successfully defending a

" wretched fortification. Nothing appears to be more contrary to sound rules
" of war, than that a Commander of garrison should risk a battle to prevent
" his being shut up and besieged. Considering, too, that his troops were sickly,
" and the army of M. de Levis well-conditioned and of triple numbers, it
" certainly was the rashest resolve that an officer, charged with the command
" of a most important fortress, could have entertained."

After reading the above, I am doubtful if many soldiers, at least at the
present day, would answer without hesitation " To be sure," to General
Murray's question. The critical moment of attack was probably made use of,
as Murray, perceiving the Chevalier advancing in single column, proceeded to
attack him before he could properly form. The disaster of the day may also
be attributed to the action of the right. The ardor of the troops carried them
further in pursuit than prudence should have dictated, and tho' they succeeded
in the commencement, they met with a severe check. The force taking
possession of the redoubts defended them with great determination, but were
eventually outnumbered and forced to retire. The left also gave way, and
Murray, driven back on both flanks, had no alternative but to seek shelter
within the walls of his fortress. On the whole he seems to have fought his
battle bravely, but the vital mistake lay in fighting at all.

The same night, M. de Levis commenced his trenches before Quebec, but
Murray, by extraordinary exertions, succeeded in mounting a number of guns,
and when the French batteries opened on the 11th of May, they were silenced
by the fire of the town. On the 15th, the English fleet, which had wintered at
Halifax, arrived at Point Levis, and having captured the French vessels lying
in the river, M. de Levis, in disgust, raised the siege, and retreated again on
Montreal, abandoning his military train and siege artillery. It was now the
turn of the English to take the offensive. General Amherst advanced from
Oswego with 10,000 men, and reached Montreal on the 6th of September;
Murray was already in the vicinity, and the next day Colonel Haviland arrived from Isle-aux-Noix. The Marquis de Vaudreuil, despairing therefore of
his ability to stand a siege, demanded a capitulation, which was granted, and
this ending the war, Canada became a British Province.

Read in connection with the accounts of the campaign, I think that
these two letters of General Murray add something to the history of the stirring times in which they were written ; and I trust they may prove acceptable
to the Literary and Historical Society of Quebec, who, I know, are anxious to
record and preserve all the waifs and strays of literature, pertaining to the
history of their ancient town.

General Murray seems to have been a brave and skilful soldier, and tho'
he committed an error of judgment in fighting at Sillery, his services, during
the campaign, were not only praiseworthy, but even brilliant. His military
talent and fertility in resource eminently qualified him for the command
of a fortress in a state of siege ; and his defence of Fort St. Philip, in Minorca,
which he held six months against the French and Spaniards, entitle him
to a distinguished place amongst the Generals of his day. His personal
character for honor stands no less high ; for when, in 1781, the Duke de Crillon,

endeavoured to bribe him with £100,000, and rank and command in the French or Spanish army, he replied in the words of the Duke's ancestor " L'honneur me le défend."

COLIN MACKENZIE,

Capt.

49, Pall Mall—London, England,

12 Nov. 1877.

P. S.—I find that Burke's Peerage, gives the sum as £100,000, and in quoting General Murray's letter to the Duke omits the retort I have given above.

F

[See Page 39.]

SIR JAMES CRAIG.

(1759-1812.)

One of our striking historical figures, whose features will doubtless in the future, assume a less repulsive aspect than that lent to it by the fiery spirits of 1810. A writer, never suspected of "anglification," Mr. P. A. DeGaspé, in his Mémoires, page 346, courageously bears testimony in favor of Sir James, Governor, of his day. Sir James Craig was undoubtedly misled in his estimate of the French element at Quebec by his very able but irresponsible advisers. The sturdy old soldier, like his great contemporary, Napoleon I, believed in bayonets, grape and canister, as educators and monitors to the *oi polloi*, on extreme occasions. That he was a bad man at heart, Mr. DeGaspé does not believe, and the generous though earnest sentiments which light up his famous Proclamation of the 21st March, 1810, favoring this view, are worthy of being preserved. " Is it for myself that I should oppress you ? Is it from ambition? what can you give me ? Is it for power? alas! my good friends, with a life ebbing out slowly to its period, under the pressure of disease acquired in the service of my country, I look only to pass what it may please God to suffer to remain of it, in the comfort of retirement among my friends. I remain among you only in obedience to the commands of my King. What power can I wish for? Is it then for wealth, that I would oppress you ? Enquire of those who know me whether I regard wealth ; I never did when I could enjoy it ; it is now of no use to me ; to the value of your country laid at my feet, I would prefer the consciousness of having, in a single instance, contributed to your happiness and prosperity."

(Christie's *History of Canada*, Vol. 1, P. 319.)

G

[See Page 40.)

LORD ELGIN'S VALEDICTORY ADDRESS.

The following affords a fair specimen of the pleasing style of oratory of the Earl of Elgin, on quitting Monklands, Montreal, at one time the seat of Government. Lord Elgin in a very felicitous manner alludes to the painful scenes of riot, &c., consequent on his courageous attitude, when called on to carry out the views of his constitutional advisers. "For nearly eight years, at the command of our beloved Queen, I have filled this position among you, discharging its duties, often imperfectly, never carelessly, or with indifference. We are all of us aware that the period is rapidly approaching when I may expect to be required by the same gracious authority to resign into other, and I trust worthier, hands the office of Governor General, with the heavy burden of responsibility and care which attaches to it. It is fitting, therefore, that we should now speak to each other frankly and without reserve. Let me assure you, then, that the severance of the formal tie which binds us together will not cause my earnest desire for your wellfare and advancement to abate. The extinction of an official relationship cannot quench the conviction that I have so long cherished, and by which I have been supported through many trials, that a brilliant future is in store for British North America; or diminish the interest with which I shall watch every event which tends to the fulfilment of this expectation. And again, permit me to assure you, that when I leave you, be it sooner or later, I shall carry away no recollections of my sojourn among you, except such as are of a pleasing character. I shall remember and remember with gratitude, the cordial reception I met with at Montreal when I came a stranger among you, bearing with me for my sole recommendation the commission of our sovereign. I shall remember those early months of my residence here, when I learnt in this beautiful neighbourhood to appreciate the charms of a bright Canadian winter day, and to take delight in the cheerful music of your sleigh bells. I shall remember one glorious afternoon—an afternoon in April—when, looking down from the hill at Monklands, on my return from transacting business in your city, I beheld that the vast plain stretching out before me, which I had always seen clothed in the white garb of winter, had assumed, on a sudden, and as if by enchantment, the livery of spring; while your noble St. Lawrence, bursting through his icy fetters, had begun to sparkle in the sunshine and to murmur his vernal hymn of thanksgiving to the bounteous Giver of light and heat. I shall remember my visits to your Mechanics' Institutes and Mercantile Library Associations, and the kind attention with which the advice which I tendered to your young men and citizens was received by them. I shall remember the undaunted courage with which the merchants of this city, while suffering under the pressure of a commercial crisis of almost unparalleled severity, urged forward that great work which was the first step towards placing Canada in her proper position in this age of railway progress. I shall remember the energy and patriotism which gathered together in this city specimens of Canadian industry, from all parts of the Province for the World's Fair, and which has been the means of rendering the magnificent conception of the illustrious Consort of our beloved Queen more serviceable to Canada than it has, perhaps, proved to any other of the countless communities which have been represented there. And I shall forget—but no—what I might have had to forget is forgotten already, and therefore I cannot tell you what 1 shall forget."

(*Letters and Journals of James, Eighth Earl of Elgin,*

Edited by Theo. Walrond, 1875.)

H.

[See Page 41.]

To His Most Excellent Majesty, George The Third, by the Grace of God, of the United Kingdom of Great Britain and Ireland, King, Defender of the Faith :

May it please Your Majesty :

The Humble Petition of Your Majesty's Faithful subjects of the Congregation of the Church of Scotland, in the City of Quebec, in the Province of Lower Canada,—

Humbly Sheweth :

That Your Majesty's Petitioners having been educated in the Principles of the Church of Scotland, and being attached to the form of Worship and the Rites and Ceremonies as established in that Church, have supported and paid during the last thirty-six years, a Minister regularly ordained of the Church of Scotland to perform public worship for them, though as your Petitioners have not had any appropriate place of Worship, nor any particular fund from whence to draw the necessary expense, they have been reduced to the necessity of an annual subscription for that purpose, which, besides being subject to variation, they consider as an improper mode of support for a Church.

That your Petitioners have always had in view to build a decent, plain Church for their public Worship, but as in such an undertaking, they expected they would be obliged to depend principally on their own resources, they have been, from several reasons and circumstances, compelled to defer it.

Your Petitioners, judging the period of the restoration of Peace (1802), favorable to their plan, have resolved to make the attempt, and they have hopes that, with a very little assistance, they may now attain the great object of their wishes—a decent place appropriated to Public Worship. Your Petitioners desire to be known to Your Majesty, and to be considered by Your Majesty's Government as members of and united to the National Church of Scotland. Your Petitioners therefore kindly hope, from Your known regard and zeal for all the Interests of true Religion, that they may receive some small mark of Your Majesty's attention and favor, to assist them in their purpose of providing a place for their Public Worship which may appear respectable to their sister Church of England, and to their fellow citizens, the Roman Catholics.

Your Majesty's Petitioners, after much inquiry, find that it will be extremely difficult to procure a convenient and reputable situation on which to build their Church, and as there is a great extent of waste ground within the walls of this City, belonging to Your Majesty, they pray that Your Majesty will be graciously pleased to favor them with a grant of a small spot of it in a convenient situation for that purpose, and Your Petitioners humbly beg leave to point out the site of the old Jesuit's Church, as a proper place, with a small extent around it to form an enclosure to protect the Building from injury or insult, and they have therefore taken the liberty to annex a Plan or Diagram of the whole of the Jesuits Garden, should any other part of it be deemed more proper or less useful to Government.

Your Petitioners beg leave to represent to Your Majesty that among the troops stationed from time to time by Your Majesty to garrison the City, and particularly in the Royal Regiment of Artillery, there are many natives of Scotland and Ireland who desire to join with Your Petitioners in Public Worship, according to the manner and form in which they have been educated—and Your Petitioners, with great satisfaction, have always endeavoured to accommodate as many of them as their present place of Public Worship permitted. But Your Petitioners, in the Church they now propose to build, intend to allot a considerable space for the express purpose of accommodating the Troops, as Your Petitioners humbly beg leave to suggest that the exercises of Public Worship are likely to be performed with most benefit, when they are conducted in the manner, and according to the forms to which the parties have been accustomed from their infancy, and they conceive it to be particularly necessary in the present times, when irreligion so much prevails, to strengthen, by every means, all those habits and customs which attach Men to Religion, and to established forms of Worship. Your Petitioners acknowledge the indulgence of Your Majesty's Governors of this Province, who have permitted them, for many years, to perform their Public Worship in the Room appointed for holding the Courts of Justice, and they beg leave to express their gratitude to Your Majesty for Your Majesty's bounty, which, by the favor of Your Majesty's Lieutenant-Governor, His Excellency, Sir Robert Shore Milnes, Baronet, has been lately extended to their present Minister, of fifty pounds per annum, as a salary to assist in supporting the respectability of their Clergyman in the Society.

Your Petitioners beg leave further humbly to submit to Your Majesty, their hopes that Your Majesty may be graciously pleased to favour them with a grant of a certain part or portion of some of the reserved lots in the Townships already granted of the waste lands of the Crown in this Province, or from any other part of these waste lands, as to Your Majesty shall appear most proper; to be vested in the Ministers and Church-Wardens, or the Ministers and Vestry of the Presbyterian Church of Scotland of the City of Quebec, and their successors-in-trust, for the purpose of raising a stipend or Salary for the

Minister or Ministers of that Church, and for such other purposes relating to that Church, as may be considered necessary to the respectability of the Public Worship performed there. As Your Majesty has freely granted to many indi-viduals large tracts of these waste lands, Your Petitioners presume to hope that Your Majesty may consider a small portion of these waste lands will be properly bestowed, when granted for the maintenance of a Branch of a National Church, acknowledged and protected by Your Majesty.

And Your Petitioners, as in duty bound, shall ever pray, &c., &c.

(*Alex. Sparks, Minister, and* 147 *others.*)

I.

[See Page 46.]

CHIEF JUSTICE SEWELL.

(1776-1839.)

Chief Justice Jonathan Sewell was born 6th June, 1766, died Nov. 12th, 1839 ; His wife, Henrietta, was the youngest daughter of Chief Justice Smith of Quebec born 6th February, 1776, died, 26th May, 1849.

HON W. SMITH.

(1769-1847.)

William Smith was second son of Chief Justice William Smith, of Quebec, born, on 7th February, 1769, educated at Kensington Grammar School, Lon-don, and came to Canada with his father in 1786. He was appointed soon after Clerk of the Provincial Parliament, and subsequently Master in Chancery of the Province of Lower Canada, and in 1814 was appointed by Earl Bathurst, a member of the Executive Council. He was the author of the "History of Canada, from its first discovery down to the year 1791." He married Susannah, daughter of Admiral Webber, and died at Quebec, 17th December, 1847.

CHIEF JUSTICE WILLIAM SMITH.

(1728-1793.)

Chief Justice William Smith was the eldest son of William Smith, who was a member of His Majesty's Council, and afterwards Judge of the Court of King's Bench for the State of New York. He was born at New York, 18th June, 1728. In his youth he was sent to a grammar school, and afterwards to Yale College, Connecticut, where he greatly distinguished himself by his learning. He was an excellent Greek and Hebrew scholar, and a thorough mathematician. He was appointed Chief Justice of New York, 24th April, 1780. At the breaking out of the rebellion in 1775, he was a staunch Loyalist, and left New York in the same vessel with the King's troops and Sir Guy

Carleton, and landed at Plymouth, 10th January, 1784. As a reward for his loyalty he was made Chief Justice of Lower Canada, 1st September 1785, and came to Canada in the Frigate " Thistle " of 28 guns, with Lord Dorchester, the Governor-General of Canada, landing at Quebec 23rd October 1786. Chief Justice Smith was the author of the " History of the Province of New York, from the first settlement down to the year 1732." He married, 3rd November, 1752, Janet, daughter of James Livingston, Esq., of New York, and died at Quebec, 6th December, 1793. His Royal Highness Prince Edward fourth son of King George III, with a numerous train of friends, followed the corpse to the grave.

E. B. TEMPLE.

Quebec, 9th December, 1880.

J.

[See Page 50.]

LIEUT-COLONEL C. CAMPBELL.

(1792-1872.)

" Lt.-Colonel Campbell, late of the old 99th Regiment of Foot (Prince of Wales, Regt.), died at his residence at Bampcell, in the Township of Halifax Megantic, on Monday the 11th instant in the 80th year of his age. He was descended from the good old U. E. L., stock, who abandoned everything for their loyalty to their Sovereign. He served with distinction during the last war on the American frontier, and was engaged in several actions on and about Lake Champlain, and at Niagara, where he was taken prisoner by an overwhelming force of Americans under the late General Winfield Scott. He always spoke in the highest terms of the kindness he experienced from his captors while in their hands. After retiring from the army, he resided for many years at Quebec, where he engaged in mercantile pursuits. Spending much of his time at the coves, his wonderful expertness as a swimmer enabled him, at various times, to save many valuable lives, the number whom he thus rescued exceeding fourteen, as we are credibly informed. The latter years of his life were spent in retirement on the borders of Lake William.—*Chronicle*, November, 1872.

K.

[See page 57.]

THE EARL OF SELKIRK.

" Thomas Douglas—fifth Earl of Selkirk, Baron Daer and Shortcleugh, Fellow of the Royal Society—was born in June, 1771, and lived an eventful life of forty-nine years. The family seat of St. Mary's Isle, in Kirkcudbright-shire, Scotland, at the mouth of the Dee, knew him but little in his adventurous career. He was an author, a patriot, a colonizer, and a philanthropist. Of a perfervid race, he was distinguished for enthusiastic devotion to his projects. The intrepidity of the Douglases, the perseverance of the ancient family of Mar, and the venturesomeness of the house of Angus, were all his inheritance by blood descent."—(*Bryce*.)

It would take a volume to follow the footsteps of this enthusiastic and clever Scot in his projects of colonization and aggrandisement in the North-West, which in the end brought much persecution and litigation on him. He died at Pau, in the Pyrenees, in 1820.

L.

[See page 59.]

The following is a list of some of Montreal's Scotch citizens of the Past and present, all of whom, as far as can be ascertained from reliable information were born in Scotland, came to this country, have been or are citizens of Montreal, and have taken active parts in the affairs of their times:—

PRESENT.

A.	Sir Hugh Allan, Andrew Allan, Chas. Alexander, R. B. Angus Robert Anderson.
B.	James Burns, Alex. Buntin.
C.	Dr. G. W. Campbell, Judge Cross, Professor J. Campbell, Jas. Court, James Croil.
D.	Wm. Darling, Geo. Denholm, George Drummond.
E.	Robert Esdaile.
F.	Hon'ble James Ferrier.
G.	David Greenshields.
H.	Jonathan Hodgson.
J.	James Johnston.
K.	Wm. Kinloch.
L.	D. Law, Rev. Gavin Lang, Archdeacon Leach.
M.	H. E. Montgomerie, Joseph Mackay, J. G. McKenzie, Henry Morgan, Ewen McLennan, Hon. D. A. MacDonald (ex Lt.-Gov. Ontario, now living in Montreal), Robt. Mitchell, John Mitchell, Alex. Mitchell, Principal D. H. MacVicar, Professor J. C. Murray, David Morrice, Edward MacKay, Duncan McIntyre, Rev. A. B. MacKay.
N. O. P.	W. J. Patterson.
R.	Andw. Robertson, R. J. Reekie, Judge T. K. Ramsay, Peter Redpath.
S.	John Sinclair, Geo. Stephen, Hon. D. A. Smith, James Stewart (*Herald*), John Sterling.
U.	Alex. Urquhart.

PAST.

A.	Robt. Armour, John Armour, George Auld.
B.	John Boston, Walter Benny, Rev. Dr. Black.
C.	Thos. Cringan, Andrew Cowan.
D.	Geo. Dempster, Wm. Dow, David Davidson.
E.	Wm. Edmonstone, Rev. H. Esson.
F.	Wm. Fraser, M.D., Adam Ferrie, James Moir Ferres.
G.	Robt. Gillespie (uncle), Robt. Gillespie (nephew), F. Gilmour, Wm. Gunn, B. R. of Montreal.
H.	Archd. Hume, A. Hall, M.D.
I. J. K.	David Kinnear, *Herald.*
L.	James Leslie, James Low, Sir Wm. Logan, James Logan.
M.	John McKenzie, James Millar, Neil Macintosh, W. G. Mack, Hon'ble Peter McGill, Hon. W. Morris, Hon. T. Mackay, Rev. Dr. Mathieson (St. Andrew's Church), Hon. James McGill.
N. O. P.	Wm. Peddie, John Orr.
R.	Donald Ross, Hew Ramsay, Wm. Ritchie, John Redpath, Dr. Robertson, Andrew Robertson, Q.C., Chief Justice Reid. Colin Russel, Geo. Rhynas, Hon. John Richardson.
S.	Andrew Shaw, John Smith, Alex. Simpson Robert Simpson, Sir George Simpson.
T.	John Torrance, David Torrance,
W.	Geo. D. Watson, Wm. Watson, Robert Weir.
Y.	Hon'ble John Young.

BRITISH OFFICERS WHO HAVE MARRIED IN CANADA.

(List made up until departure of troops, 1871.)

Rifle Brigade.

Earl of Errol ...... Miss Gore

7th Hussars.

Col. White .... Miss DeMontenach
Major Campbell... " Duchesnay

13th Hussars.

Capt. Clarke ...... Miss Rose
Capt. Joyce ...... " Austen
Lieut. Miles ...... " Esten
Dr. Milburn ...... " Allan

Royal Artillery.

Col. Shakspear ... Miss Panet
" Pipon .... " Ashworth
" FitzGerald ... " LeMoine
" Clifford ...... " LeMesurier
" Walker ...... Mrs. Ball
" Haultain..... Miss Gordon
" De Winton... " Rawson
" Burrows ..... " Cronyn
Capt. Noble . .... " Campbell
" Farmer ..... " DeBlaquiere
" Farmer ..... " Farrrell
" Turner...... " Widder

78

Dr. Duff .... Miss Sewell
Capt. Brackenbury. " Campbell
Dr. McIntosh..... " Wood
Lieut. Irwin ..... " Hamilton
" A. W. White. " Young
" Appleby ... " MacDonald
" Sandilands . " Stevenson
" Brown ..... " Kirkpatrick
Capt. Hotham.... " Hale
" Turner..... " Gzowski
' Sandham .. " Maria Gzowski
Col. Mackay ..... " Wood

Royal Engineers.

Col. Gallwey.... Miss McDougall
" Brown ...... " Hunt
Col. Ford........ " Racey
" White ...... " Gibson
" Beatson .... " Gordon
" Murray ..... " Fisher
Capt. Noble ...... " Lunn
" DeMontmorency " Motz
" Mann .... " Geddes
" Burnaby .... " Felton
" Jervois...... " Napier
" Farrell...... " Jarvis
Lieut. Carlisle.... " Phillips
" Savage .... " Joly
" Turner .... " Sprague
" Hon. Bury . " Austin

Grenadier Guards.

Lord Abinger .... Miss Macgruder
Capt. Herbert .... " LeMoine
Dr. Girdwood .... " Blackwell

Coldstream Guards.

Capt. Clayton ...... Miss Wood
" Kirkland ..... " Paterson

1st Dragoon Guards.

Capt. Mills......... Miss Hatt

1st Royals.

Capt. Davenport..... Miss Sewell
" McNicoll ..... " Wood

13th Hussars.

Capt. Clay .... Miss Buchanan
Lieut. Moore .... " Ostell

7th Royal Fusiliers.

Capt. W. Pryce Brown. Miss Prior
Lieut. Winter .... " Sewell

9th Regiment.

Capt. Straubenzee ... Miss Cartwright
" Terry......... " Taylor

15th Regiment.

Lieut.-Col. Nash..... Miss Nanton
Major Temple ...... " Sewell
" Eden......... " Caldwell

16th Regiment.

Major Lucas .... Miss McKenzie
" Baker .... " Cunningham
Capt. Carter .... " LeMesurier
" Lea .... " Alloway
" Platt.......... " Howard
Dr. Ferguson........ " Alloway
Lieut. Kane......... " Coursol

17th Regiment.

Capt. Heigham...... Miss Fraser
" Webber .... " Jeffery
" Utterson ...... " Burstall
" Parker........ " Webster
Lieut. Burnett....... " Kreighoff
" Lees .... " Motz
" Torre .... Mrs. Stevenson
" Harris .... Miss Motz
" Presgrave ..... " Day

20th Regiment.

Col. Horne .... Miss Moore
Capt. Knight .... " Harris
Lieut. Peard........ " Harris
" Turner........ " Arnoldi
" Garstin ...... " ————

23rd Royal Welch Fusiliers.

Col. Crutchley....... Miss Harris
Capt. Willoughby.... " DeRochblave
" Hopton .... " Vaughan
Lieut. Battye....... " Walford
" Ferguson..... " Hill
" Raynes ...... " Bowman
" Holland...... " Givins
" Agassiz ...... " Schram
" Howell....... " Whitehead
" Benyon....... " Allan
" Rowley .... " Hollis
Dr. Grantham....... " Blenkarne
Dr. Browne........ " Massingbird

25th Borderers.

Capt. Smythe....... Miss Perrault
Dr. Gribben .... " Allan
Lieut. Lees .... " Maxham

26th Regiment.
Col. Crespigny .... Miss Buchanan

29th Regiment.
Col. Middleton ...... Miss Doucet
Capt. Phipps........ " Geddes

30th Regiment.
Col. Atcherley .... Miss Heward
Capt. Moorson ..... " McCutcheon
Capt. Birch .... " Vass
Dr. Paxton.......... " Murray
" Hooper .... " Dalkin
Capt. Clarkson ...... " Coxwell
" Glascott....... " Cayley
" Nagle .... " Bell
Lieut. Flemming .... " Sewell
" Charlewood ... " Poston

32nd Regiment.
Dr. M. Healey ...... Miss Smith

39th Regiment.
Capt. Dixon .... Miss Antrobus
" Hawtayne .... " Healey
" Tryon .... " McLeod
Lieut. Osborne Smith. " Smith
" Hoare .... " Scott

47th Regiment.
Lieut.-Col. Villiers...Miss Shanly
Capt. Larken........ " Savage
" Berckley ...... " Dixon
Dr. Jamieson .... " Cartwright
Lt. de J. Prevost...... " Dow
Ens. Dixon.......... " McMurray

53rd Regiment.
Capt. Brown........Miss DeWar
Lieut. Hitchcock..... " Ferguson

54th Regiment.
Capt. Lake.......... Miss Phillips
" Thompson...... " Boxer

56th Regiment.
Capt. Austin........Miss Goff

60th Rifles.
Capt. LeBreton.......Miss George
" Hamilton....... " Willan
" Travers........ " Johnson

Capt. Henderson ..... Miss Starnes
" Worseley ...... " Sicotte
" Northey ...... " Gzowski
" Crosby........ " Thompson
Lieut. Mitchell Innes. " Starnes

63rd Regiment.
Col. Hon. Dalzell ....Miss Harris

66th Regiment.
Col. Dames......... Miss Kemble
Capt. Serocold........ " Duval
Capt. Torrens........ " Price
Lieut. Godby .... " DesFossés
Dr. Henry .... " Geddes
Lieut. Cunningham .. " Robertson

68th Regiment.
Col. Rhodes.......... Miss Dunn
Capt. Durnford....... " Sewell
Capt. Barlow........ " Boxer
Lieut. Brown........ " Stevenson

69th Regiment.
Capt. Clarke........
" Thorpe.......Miss Jeffery
Lieut. Homes ......
Lieut. Glendonwyn...Miss Chauveau.

70th Regiment.
Gen. Evans, C.B...... Miss Ogden
Major Taylor .... " Andrews

71st Regiment.
Major Denny...... Miss Richardson
Capt. Scott......... " Stayner
" Ready....... " Hincks
" E. Antrobus.. " Bréhaut
" Hanson ..... " Brehaut
Lieut. Orde........ " Jarvis

73rd Regiment.
Lieut. Fitzgerald....Miss Hamilton

74th Regiment.
Capt. Austin...... Miss Hall

78th Highlanders.
Capt. Colin McKenzie Miss Falkenberg
Capt. Fraser....... Miss Dupont

79th Cameron Highlanders.
Col. Butt......... Miss Sewell

Major Ross........Miss Lindsay
Capt. Cummings.... " Coxworthy
" Reeve .... " Fraser

82nd Regiment.

Capt. Puleston..... " Scharm
" Diggle....... " Holman

89th Regiment.

Capt. Collingwood .Miss Maxwell
Lieut. Isaacs....... " Cartwright
" Shuter ...... " Taylor

93rd Sutherland Highlanders.

Lieut. Elliott....... Miss Wood

100th Regiment.

Capt. Herring......Miss L. Bell
Lieut. Latouche .... " Bouchette

Rifle Brigade.

Capt. Glynn .... Miss Dewar
" Kingscote..... " Stuart
" Dalzel........ " Harris
" Swaine........ " Reynolds
Lieut. Swann .... " Price
" Dillon .... .. " Stanton
Dr. Hunt........... " Jeffery
" Walters........ " Geddes

R. Canadian Rifles.

Col. Moffatt........Miss Buchanan
" Walker .... " Yule
Major Bernard...... " Kingsmill
" Bernard,1st wife " Jarvis
" Holmes ...... " Morris
" Hibbard ..... " O'Hara
Capt. Gibson........ " Gibb
" Dunn .... " Gibb
" Clarke........ " Heward
" Weyland ..... " ———
Lieut. Innes........ " Clarke
" Money....... " Buckley
" Pechell ...... " ———

Lieut. Lowe ....Miss Gemley
" Arnott....... " Jones

Royal Navy.

Sir J. Westphall.....Mrs. Gore
Commander Ashe....Miss Percy
Capt. Orlebar........ " Hale
" Bayfield........ " Wright
" Greer......... " Kimber
Lieut. Story......... " Murray
Mr. Knight.......... " Poetter

Commissariat Department.

Com. Gen. Smith....Miss Goddard
" Price..... " Jones
" Davenport. " McNab
" Lundy.... " Askin
" Bower.... " Bradbury
" Walcott .. " Adamson
" Weir ..... " Stayner
Dep.-Com. Coxworthy. " Goddard
Dep.- Com. Webb.... " Bradshaw
Sir Randolph Routh .. " Taschereau
Dep.-Com.-Gen. Routh " Hall
Dep.-Com.-Gen. Leonce
Routh .... " Pardey
Assist.-Dep.-Com,-Gen.
Price............. " Boston

Staff.

Col. Pritchard.... Miss De Montenach
" Eden .... " Prentice

Medical Staff.

Dr. McCabe......... Mrs. Lewis
" Woodman.......Miss Stevenson
" Hacket......... " Uniacke
" Henry .... " Geddes
" Blatherwick ..... " White

Ordnance.

Major Holwell. ...... Miss Gibson
Lieut. Bligh......... " Whale

Mr. B. Sulte, of Ottawa, contributes as follows :

MARRIAGES.

Canadien du 26 décembre 1808.

" A Québec, le 16 de ce mois, le Capt. John Flack, des Royaux Vétérans, à Demoiselle M. A. Ang. Cuvillier.

Canadien du 23 septembre 1809.

" Marié, le ₁9, Capt. Edw. Dewar, Aide-de-Camp de Son Excellence le Gouverneur-en-Chef, à Demoiselle Maria Longmore, de cette ville."

Marié le 26 décembre 1809, le Colonel H. Zouch, du 10e Batt. des Vétérans Royaux, à Demoiselle Ann Ritchie, nièce de Ralp. Gray, Ecr. M.P.P. pour le Comté de Québec.—(*Canadien* du 6 Janvier 1810.)

Ethnological Notes, from Church Registers illustrative of alliances between Canadians of French descent and persons of Scotch and other descent :—

A.

Archer—Lamontagne
Amiot—Billingsley
Amiot—Pennée
Aumond—McCord

B.

Bouchette—Fraser
Bouchette—Williams
Bouchette—Gardiner
Bouchette—Lindsay
Bouchette—Shea
Bouchette—Hart
Bouchette—Neilson
Bouchette—Latouche
Bouchette—Cummings
Bouchette—Barthelet
Bouchette—Evans
Bossé—Hullett
Bourret—Lindsay
Bedard—Marret
Blanchet—Seymour
Bruneau—Scott
Blanchet—Balzaretti.
Beaudry—Burroughs
Baby—Cannon

C.

Carrier—Sheppard
Caron—Fitzpatrick
Cauchon—Nowlan
Carrier—Donaghue
Casault—Pangman
Chauveau—Glendonwyn
Chauveau—Maher

D.

DeLanaudiere—Young
DeLanaudiere—Selby
DeLery—Alleyn
DeSalaberry—Hatt
Duchesnay—Wotherspoon
Duchesnay—Gugy
Duchesnay—Dunn
Duchesnay—Bradbury
Duchesnay—Campbell
Duchesnay—Prevost
Duchesnay—Sharples
DeGaspé—Alison
DeGaspé—Power
DeGaspé—Stuart
DeGaspé—Alleyn
DeGaspé—Fraser
DeGaspé—Fraser
Drolet—Neilson
Drolet—Motz
Drolet—Laurie
Doucet—Middleton
Desfossés—Goadby
Duberger—Glackmeyer
DesRivières—McCord
DeLongueuil—Grant
DeLongueuil—Grant
Desbarats—Pemberton
Desbarats—Pemberton
Desbarats—Selby
Desbarats—Smith
DeBellefeuille—Lindsay
Duberger—Slevin
Duberger—Nesbitt

E

Evanturel—Lee
Evanturel—Lee

F

Faribault—Anderson
Frémont—Scott
Fiset—Powers
Fiset—Morrison

G

Guéroult—Lindsay
Garneau—Burroughs
Guéroult—Lemesurier
Guy—Pemberton
Guichard—Dunn

H.

Hamel—Campbell
Hubert—Neilson

J.

Juste—Vanfelson

L.

LaCorne—Lennox
Langevin—Armstrong
Langevin—Armstrong
Langevin—Little
Langevin—Phillips
Langevin—McLean
Langevin—Furniss
Laterrière—Bulmer
Laterrière—Slevin
Languedoc—Prinschikoff
Larue—Church
Larue—Burroughs.
LeMoine—McPherson
LeMoine—Lindsay
LeMoine—Melvin
LeMoine—Woolsey
LeMoine—McPherson
LeMoine—Warrick
LeMoine—Maxham
LeMoine—FitzGerald
LeMoine—Atkinson

LeMoine—Herbert
LeMoine—Stimson
LeMoine—Brigham
LeMoine—Mackay
LeVasseur—Smith
Lamontagne—Lee
Langlois—McDonald
Leblond—Jackson
Lamotte—Bell
LeSage—Pemberton
Lotbiniere—Munro

M.

Massue—Marret
Montenach—Pritchard
Mondelet—Carter
Mondelet—Smith
Mason—McKenzie

P.

Panet—Blake
Polette—McCord
Panet—Harwood
Paré—Slevin
Pinsonnault—Hallowell
Perrault—Lindsay
Perrault—Ryan

S.

Sicotte—Worseley
Savard—Slevin
Savard—Lee

T.

Taschereau—Routh
Taschereau—Ross
Taschereau—Pentland
Taschereau—Charlton
Taschereau—Harwood
Taschereau—Alleyn
Tessier—McKenzie
Tessier—Kelly
Turcotte—McDonald

V.

Voyer—Burroughs
Verret—Shehyn

Some explanations may not be out of place in order to understand the above short tabular statement, relative to alliances in a few of the best known families. Starting with the illustrous old house of Longueuil we have the widow and the daughter of the third Baron de Longueuil, merging their baronial name in that of Grant; a warlike LaCorne espouses a proud Lennox of the ducal house of Richmond, Gordon and Aubigny, whilst a successful French Canadian politician, the Hon. Joseph Cauchon Lieutenant-Governor of Manitoba, carried off to the Prairie Province his devoted and accomplished Irish wife, Miss Mary Nowlan of Edgehill Sillery, alas! no more. A family, high in the Church and on the Bench, the Taschereau, contract six *unfrench* alliances, the first with Sir Randolph Routh ; the Hon. M. de Sales de Laterrière, marries the daughter of Sir Henry Bulmer of London. The daughter of a late Premier of Ontario Hon. J. Sandfield McDonald becomes the spouse of a late Member for Montmorency, Jean Langlois, Esq., whilst the daughter of a late Premier of Quebec, Hon. P. J. O. Chauveau, is united to a British Officer, Lt. Glendonwyn, and a rising young Irish barrister Chs. Fitzpatrick, finds a bride in the family of a late Lieutenant-Governor of Quebec, the Hon. R. E. Caron, The Langevins join hands with the Armstrongs, Philips, McLeans, Furniss, &c., and the DeGaspes, with the Allisons, Frasers, Stuarts, Powers, Alleyns, etc.,

It would take us much beyond the limits prescribed, to pursue in detail this curious study, of the doings of that irrepressible Divinity, yclept Hymen; we shall close by calling attention to the names on this list of no less than, eleven sages of our Bench, viz. : Hon. Justice Bedard, Bossé, Casault, Fiset Mondelet, McCord, Power, Polette, Stuart, Tessier, Vanfelson, all united, as appears on reference to the above, to mates of descent other than that of their ermined Lords. Future searchers of history and Church Registers, will doubtless yet add considerably to the ethnological labours of such arduous and successful toilers as the Abbès Ferland, Tanguay and Langevin.

THE END